Dedication

To my Mum
To my Dad

But Most of All to my Husband
Without whom none of this would have been possible

"Some names of people, places and horses have been changed"

CHAPTER 1

'She's gone back to the dealer's.'
I felt my stomach lurch and something close to panic rising in my throat.

'Gone back to the dealer's? When?'

'Yesterday. We couldn't keep her; she's not a riding school horse.'

My mind went into freefall. Oh no! Oh no! Then I thought... not a riding school horse... what on earth do they mean by that?

I always said that I would never buy a horse; I didn't want a horse, I knew nothing about horses, but I had always loved them. As a child I was nuts about them. And, if I'm perfectly honest, I was also a little frightened of them – they intimidated me with their sheer size and strength. Yet I was drawn to them like a ping-pong ball on a piece of elastic, always bouncing back and powerless to resist.

My first memory of a horse was as a young child living in a small semi in Northolt. One day, I was sitting in our living room at the back of the house when I heard a deep voice echoing in the street outside. A strange jumble of words came tumbling through the gaps in our draughty windows and floated down the hallway, like smoke from a genie's lamp.

'What's that man saying, Mum?' I asked, intrigued.

'Oh, that's the rag-and-bone man, dear, with his horse and cart,' she said.

The sing-song voice beckoned again and I ran to our front room, ducked my head under the flimsy net curtain and flattened my nose against the window pane. I watched in silent wonder as a magnificent black horse walked sedately by, pulling a flat, wooden cart in its wake. I stared at him clip-clopping along; the shaggy, long, 'feathered' hair around his legs flaring out from his knees like bell-bottom trousers, the arch of his neck accentuated by rippling muscles and a flowing black mane, and his deep, powerful, ebony chest encircled by a shiny, black leather harness with polished brass buckles. Mesmerised, I stood rooted to the spot, wiping the misted glass with my fingers as condensation from two hot streams of breath squeezed from my nostrils and threatened to obscure the view.

And that, as they say, was that. During this first brief encounter, something within my young and impressionable body happened at a molecular level and the imprint of that horse stamped itself indelibly on my genes. It was love at first sight; and like all first loves, was never forgotten.

As a skinny youngster growing up, there was never any spare money in my parents' household, so regular riding lessons were out of the question. My only contact with horses was through books, the TV or the odd riding lesson bought as a Christmas or birthday present. But I drew the short straw on these last two events as both occurred in the dark and dismal month of December, when I usually ended up either soaked to the skin or freezing my socks off.

My parents always used to say, 'When you're older and earning your own money you'll be able to pay for proper riding lessons, dear.'

Yeah, yeah, yeah, I would think, feeling deprived.

The 1960s left me feeling restless as my teenage years came and went, along with various boyfriends. Suffocated by the rules of conventionality that straight-jacketed women into the roles of teacher, nurse or secretary, I departed our staid shores for the unknown exotica of foreign travel. Throughout my twenties and thirties I worked overseas in a motley selection of jobs, none of which were permanent or paid enough to satisfy a mortgage lender. I picked olives on the hillsides of Greece, tended tomatoes and cucumbers by the sea, lived life to the full under a hot Cretan sun, answerable to no one but myself. Amidst this heady mix of socialising, irregular hours, no responsibilities and spur of the moment decisions, the longed-for riding lessons never materialised.

As with all things, even perfection loses its allure when only compared to itself and after fifteen years I became tired of my bohemian lifestyle. I yearned for the conventional: job, house, marriage and 2.4 kids (well, those were the statistics when I was young), and with the added incentive that 'women' and 'careers' had become more willing bedfellows, I decided to entrust my future to the grey skies of my homeland. I found a reasonable job in the UK, which hinted at prospects, and was welcomed back to the fold by my parents, with open arms.

I was 40, single, with no ties and a modicum of solvency. Yet after work I would rattle around the house on my own, with time on my hands and a feeling of emptiness in my gut.

'You need a hobby; something to keep you occupied, something you enjoy,' came the stern advice from friends.

What do 40-year-olds do in England in their spare time I asked myself? Fulfil promises they made to themselves as a child, I thought, that's what they do. So I decided to go for the one thing I had always wanted – to learn to ride and spend time with those magnificent animals that until now I had only been able to admire from a distance.

Most people can get away with sitting on a riding school horse, bouncing about for a while until they get the hang of the 'rising' trot. Me – I wanted more than that. I wanted to be a competent rider with enough ability to enjoy a reasonable ride without scaring myself to death, or doing myself a mischief. I had no desire to ride 'lively' or 'naughty' horses, compete at shows, jump fences or tackle the technical merits of dressage. In fact, age had triumphed over the recklessness of youth and I knew my boundaries. Don't get me wrong, I never ceased to be in awe of those people who would fearlessly 'sit' on any horse. I admired their ability to react instinctively to fickle-natured beasts that could take umbrage at the most innocuous object, and I would watch from the sidelines with a secret longing, knowing that I would never have the ability, or nerve, to ride anything that wasn't virtually 'bombproof'. I wanted to ride for the sheer pleasure of it, for the partnership between man and beast and for the physical experience of being close to these animals of such beauty and grace.

Never one to do things by halves, I laid out a plan of action and set my goals. Required – one good riding school, with quality horses, beautiful countryside to ride out in, and a floodlit indoor arena for rainy days and dark evenings. Out came the telephone directory and the maps, and I was off on a mission. I drove along country lanes barely wide enough for one car, let alone two; creeping round bends with overgrown hedgerows, praying that I wouldn't meet anything coming in the opposite direction. I passed quaint pubs and even quainter villages, with names like Street End, Cop Street and Lynsore Bottom in my quest for the perfect place, and it wasn't long before I found myself outside the gates of a serious contender, deep in the Kent countryside. I pulled in and parked on the forecourt. Initial enquiries revealed nice people, great horses which were well looked after, a variety of country walks and trails to ride along, an indoor school and a floodlit outdoor arena; giving me a whole host of options for my ride without being held to ransom by the vagaries of the English weather. What more could I ask for?

I started weekly lessons, became a 'regular' and loved every minute of it. Gradually my riding skills improved, giving me confidence and a sense of purpose. Often I would take a change of clothes to work so that I could dash off to the riding school at the end of a stressful shift, and I became contented with my lot in life. I even became resigned to my single status and the slightly depressing fact that my ticking clock of motherhood was sadly past its sell-by date.

Then, just when I'd given up all hope of finding the right partner, I met Mike. We'd seen each other around at work, buzzing backwards and forwards between different departments, but we'd never really had a proper conversation until fate lent a hand and the company decided to install a new computer system. As anyone who has ever met me knows, I am a one-woman disaster zone where computers are concerned; in fact, just being in the vicinity of anything requiring 'programming' seems to produce an alarming catalogue of malfunctions.

Fed up with the endless technical problems that seemed to befall my equipment, my boss instructed me in no uncertain terms to: 'Go and liaise with the IT department!'

And liaise I did. Mike was in charge of that section, and his initial reaction to my intrusion into his busy schedule was to foist me off onto one of his colleagues. But he hadn't taken into account my adverse effect on modern technology. In the end, having driven everyone else to near distraction, Mike was forced to take charge of me himself. Sitting side by side at my computer terminal, slowly but surely Mike's eyes wandered from the keyboard to my hemline and a spark ignited.

I did try to warn him though. 'I'm not an easy person,' I parried, when he asked me out for a drink.

But he countered with, 'That should make life interesting.'

So I thought I might be in with a chance. They say opposites attract and that was certainly true in our case, for I was as impulsive and excitable as Mike was cautious and composed. To the amazement of all our colleagues, romance blossomed in that stuffy office environment and, although it was too late to have children together, Mike was in time to save me from a dotty spinsterhood and solo dining.

As we got to know each other, Mike asked about my enthusiasm for horse riding.

'Isn't it a bit dangerous… I mean, aren't you frightened of falling off?' he said hesitantly.

'Oh no,' I chided. 'All the riding school horses are so well behaved. Why don't you come along and try it out for yourself – we could book a lesson together.'

'I'll think about it,' Mike said and left me to it, showing no inclination whatsoever to take me up on my offer.

I had scoffed when colleagues asked me if I wanted to buy my own horse. The logic was there for all to see, or so I thought. I could pick and choose which days I went to the riding school. Often, in the summer when it was warm and dry, I would ride twice a week, and in the winter months with the evenings drawing in, I would book a lesson once a week or sometimes less, if the weather was very bad.

There were a couple of girls who had their own horses at the school on a 'livery' basis, where they rented a stable and grazing, which included use of the school facilities. I listened with horror to tales of mucking out stables at 6.00 a.m. before going to work. And the daily commitment of time and money seemed incomprehensible to someone as free and independent as me. As much as I loved horses, there was no way that I would ever buy my own. In my opinion those girls needed their brains testing.

How naïve my comments now seem. Yet I assured my friends that I was the sensible one. Why pay out all that money to buy my own horse and spend time and effort looking after it, when I could have just as much pleasure, probably more, by popping into the riding school each week as the mood took me?

'Personally,' I said, cake and eating it coming to mind, 'I can't imagine why anyone would want to go to all that trouble.'

Then, one morning, everything changed.

CHAPTER 2

Have you ever felt swept along by a situation; caught in the grip of an invisible force that you cannot pull back from, like water swirling down a plughole? Well, that's what happened to me when I arrived at the riding school for my usual lesson to find a grey horse I had never seen before, standing on the yard. It was all tacked up with saddle and bridle, waiting to be ridden.

As I approached, my instructor called out, 'We have a new horse for you to try out today, Gillian.'

Little did I know that this horse was about to change my life, completely and irrevocably. It was not the usual, heavier type of horse that is commonly used at riding schools, but a fine-boned, relatively small horse, a mare of around 15.1 hands high (that's roughly five foot from ground to shoulder height). And to me, she was beautiful.

'She's called Ballista, and you're riding her today.'

I had a half-an-hour private lesson and she was as sharp as a paper edge – but I thought I had the measure of her and the lesson went well. At the end of our allotted time we left the arena, and as we were walking back to the yard, something came over me. I don't know why I said it, I just did.

Mike has often accused me of opening my mouth at the wrong time and speaking without thinking things through. This is quite true and I have to hold my hands up to it. I blame my impulsive nature, over which I sometimes have no control whatsoever. However, this particular remark was to boomerang back big time.

'She's lovely,' I said. 'If I ever bought a horse, it would be something like this.'

My instructor looked at me with raised eyebrows.

'I wouldn't have put you down as someone who would buy their own horse,' she said.

'No, I'm not really,' I stuttered. 'I mean… just that… if I ever *did* buy one, this is the sort of horse that I would go for… one about this size and similar in build.'

'Actually we already have a buyer for this horse,' she responded softly. 'She's going to a lady looking for a nice, quiet mare.'

So it was only a matter of time before Ballista would be whisked away to her new home and I thought no more of it.

We were very busy at work and things were just as chaotic on the home front. Mike and I had decided to put our relationship on a firmer footing, and three months into our house-hunt a quirky bungalow with a pretty back garden took our fancy. Negotiations for the purchase went into full flow, so another two weeks sped by before I had the chance to go riding again.

But when I did, I was greeted with the words, 'Did you mean what you said last time you were here… about the grey mare?'

Taken by surprise, I hurriedly tried to think back. What did I say last time?

As if she'd read my thoughts, the proprietor said, 'About Ballista, the grey mare – that she would be just what you wanted if you were buying a horse.'

'Why?' I said. 'I thought she'd been sold.'

'Well, the lady isn't buying her now, so she's up for sale if you want her. If not I'm afraid she'll have to go back to the dealers and take her chances. You're riding her again today, so think about it.'

'Back to the dealers!' I said aghast.

The proprietor looked at me expectantly.

'I, um, don't know, really, er…' I stammered, now lost for words. 'I'll think about it and let you know.'

Think about it? My stomach suddenly started to flutter. But I don't want to buy a horse, do I? No, I don't, this is ridiculous, all because I opened my big mouth and made a stupid comment. I'll put them straight, as soon as I've had my ride.

After my ride, I spent a few moments petting the mare. For some strange reason all white horses are referred to as greys, regardless of how darkly 'dappled' or 'white' they are in reality. Although Ballista looked almost pure white from a distance, when I looked more closely, her coat was actually flecked with tiny, light brown dots, like freckles, which were rather attractive. My hand reached out instinctively to feel the warm smoothness of her coat, and fascinated by those little dots, I let my fingers slowly drift along the fine line of her neck, over her shoulders and along the curve of her back. I closed my eyes and breathed in her pungent horsey smell; a smell that people either love or hate. And as I laid my head close to her side, I was shocked to feel a tremor of excitement run right through me at the thought of this horse being mine.

'She's flea-bitten,' Jennie said, breaking my reverie.

'Flea-bitten?' I gasped, withdrawing my hand with an involuntary jerk.

'No, not literally,' she laughed, 'that's the name for this type of colouring on a horse's coat. They're known as flea-bitten greys.'

Somehow, after my lesson, I never had the opportunity to 'put them straight'. I went back to my car and tried to put this absurd thought right out of my mind, dismissing it as downright impractical and, furthermore, economically out of the question. But my brain refused to comply and took on an obstinate independence of its own. The idea nagged at me as I drove home. It continued to badger me for the rest of the afternoon, then all through dinner and into the evening. I tried to concentrate on the TV but my mind kept wandering off, until I finally gave up and went to bed. But there was no respite there either. I tossed and turned, tried to reason with myself, tried to forget – all to no avail. Nothing could stop the stream of images that flowed through my mind like stills from an old cinema screen, and I could not turn my thoughts away from this pretty mare. How many times had she already changed hands, passed from one owner to another like a parcel in a children's party game? Vulnerable to the whims of mankind, she had no choice regarding her future; could neither decide for herself, nor stand up for herself. She was just a helpless pawn in the ebb and flow of life, and that touched something deep within me. Who cared what happened to her?

… *I* cared.

In the morning, over breakfast, I decided to exorcise the idea by discussing it with Mike.

'So, the horse is for sale. So what?' he said.

I looked at him in silence. He looked back at me for what seemed like a long time and still I said nothing. Realisation was a long time dawning, but his expression subtly changed as his eyebrows rose.

'This isn't a serious question, is it?' he said.

'Well, I don't know,' was the truthful reply.

'I'm sure someone else will come along and buy her if she is as pretty as you say she is. What's more to the point, you know nothing about looking after horses,' Mike said, with more than a hint of exasperation creeping into his voice as he went on to list all the other reasons why buying a horse wasn't a sensible idea.

'I can't do this without your support,' I replied softly.

My words hung in the air and I stared at the patterned tiles on the kitchen floor, while the second hand of the wall clock slowly ticked away time.

I heard the sharp intake of Mike's breath, and ever practical, he asked, 'Well, let's have a look at the figures first… You have done the figures, haven't you?'

Done the figures? I had no idea – this came straight from the heart, but at least I could start breathing again.

'Okay, okay, what are we looking at here?' he continued. 'Where would you keep her, how much is it going to cost and do you even know how much they want for her?'

No, I didn't know the answer to any of these questions, but I sure as hell could find out.

I needed to take another trip back to the riding school – but first, I had to make a few phone calls, check out the livery yards in my area, find out what each was offering and make a few price comparisons. Not for me, you understand. I already knew that if I was going to take on the responsibility of buying a horse I needed the advice of people I knew and trusted. People who had spent their whole lives with horses: who had made their own mistakes along the way, and from whose experience I too could learn. And that was at my riding school.

But Mike looked at things differently. I knew that I would need a rock-solid financial package to get him on board and sway the balance in my favour. Then I had a brilliant idea. Maybe I could just buy her on behalf of the riding school. They could look after her and use her for lessons, which would pay for her keep and I would have the satisfaction of knowing she had a good home. As a bonus, I'd be able to ride her every week. Perfect!

My next step was to go back to the riding school to see how feasible my brilliant idea was. The response was crushing.

'But she's just not a riding school horse.'

I had no idea what this phrase meant, but I was to hear it said time and again before I finally understood the significance of it.

Unwilling to admit defeat so early on in the challenge, I realised it had to be all or nothing – not that I had completely made up my mind, as yet…

I quickly got back on track and returned to my original plan.

'Okay then, come on, how much do you want for her and what are your livery charges?' I asked.

'You do realise that the true cost of a horse isn't in the purchase price, don't you?'

No, I didn't, but tell me more, I thought.

'It's all the other expenses that add up,' the livery manager said.

Where Mike was concerned, I decided to keep that little snippet of information to myself for the time being and got down to the nitty-gritty. 'A list' was started. First of all there were the immediate expenses, such as making sure her vaccinations were up to date, having her wormed if necessary, asking the farrier to check out her feet and obtaining quotes for horse insurance. Then we started on the day-to-day expenses of keeping a horse. We went through a sliding scale of costs, depending on how much of the work I was able or willing to do myself: grass livery, full livery, do-it-yourself livery, grass livery plus stable and any number of permutations in-between.

Then there was her wardrobe… Her wardrobe?… Yes, her wardrobe. She would need a selection of rugs: lightweight, medium, heavyweight, turnout and stable as well as a sweat rug and possibly a fly or shower rug for summer. Then there was the issue of neck covers: separate or integrated, lightweight or padded, available in a variety of makes, styles, sizes and colours, all priced from economy to upmarket. In fact, the list grew to such an extent that my head was spinning and two new lists had to be started: one for 'essential items needed now' and the other for 'items to be bought later'. Essentials went on to include grooming kit, headcollar, tack, brushing boots, overreach boots… what on earth *are* all these things, I wondered to myself. I had no idea a horse needed so much gear. And then another thought occurred to me… Goodness knows what Mike will say when he sees this lot.

But something strange happened as I spent the day compiling lists and setting out a budget. Initially my glib comment was essentially just that – a remark with no substance. Yet, the more I gathered the facts and figures, the more convinced I became that this whole thing was viable and the more I wanted that horse. What had started out as an off-the-cuff remark was now becoming a tangible possibility.

CHAPTER 3

L ife's a funny old thing; some people believe that our path is already mapped out for us – others, that we make our own destiny. Whichever is true of this confusingly complex journey, I believe that everything happens for a reason. It may not be immediately obvious what that reason is, but the ripples of life events often continue to radiate outwards for years, unnoticed, like a gigantic wave slowly gathering momentum, until it finally bursts with pent-up fury upon the shore, wreaking havoc in its wake.

Shortly before I met Mike, I began having a series of apparently unconnected minor digestive ailments. With life ticking over nicely, I tried to ignore the increasingly repetitive symptoms that started to intrude into my world. But slowly and insidiously these minor mishaps merged into one larger 'mystery' illness, which hijacked my daily routine and relentlessly took charge.

I had always been fit and active but as the months progressed, my symptoms spun out of control, changing me from someone I knew into someone I didn't. I lost my confidence, became apprehensive about travelling anywhere and felt overwhelmed by fatigue and the constant need to use a loo. Finally, after a barrage of tests, the diagnosis was delivered.

In the warm, sterile confines of a hospital consulting room Mike and I looked at each other in bewilderment, 'Ulcerative colitis?'

I'd never heard of it before. What is it and what did it all mean for me?

'It's an inflammatory bowel disease,' explained the hospital consultant.

'What causes it?' I asked.

And I knew we were in trouble when he pursed his lips and replied, 'That's a million-dollar question.'

Well, if he didn't know, then who did? But at least he was honest.

My foreboding deepened when he told me that there was no cure for this condition and that the aim was to keep the symptoms under control with a range of medication.

Initially I thought that I could just pop a few pills each day and everything would resolve itself, but slowly I came to realise that medicine is not an exact science. This particular condition is as individual as patients themselves, and their responses to different types of medication can vary just as much. There was a long and difficult road ahead for both Mike and myself, and at the time, I couldn't imagine living with an illness that was to all intents and purposes incurable. Neither could I come to terms with the physical and mental effects caused by this alien condition that had stripped me of my dignity.

We searched for information, trawled the internet, made assumptions and then backtracked. We looked for clues to find a way out and then tried a different approach. We attempted to rationalise cause and effect, looked at alternative medicine, but whatever combination I tried, we always seemed to come up against a brick wall. Following my diagnosis, there were times when I felt so despondent and powerless that I believed all the opportunities life had once held in store for me had been snatched away. But I was to be proved wrong.

Whilst I had enthused over the riding facilities available at this particular school when I first made my choice of establishment, I hadn't considered the one convenience that would become crucial to the continuation of my riding. For someone with colitis, this school happened to possess the most precious commodity of all – an outside WC, which was to become my lifeline. I was determined that this illness was not going to get the better of me, and as I struggled with my symptoms, my riding became the barometer by which I gauged my return to 'normality'.

My interaction with horses made me feel close to nature, bringing a sense of peace into my soul, and I became convinced that there was a direct parallel between horses and my physical well-being.

Now, as I clutched the burgeoning list of essentials and non-essentials, I realised that owning a horse was not just a matter of time and money, but would test me both physically and mentally. As such, the purchase of this horse took on an even deeper meaning for me; placing me on a par with all the other 'normal' riders, it became the representation of my return to health.

CHAPTER 4

Mike and I sat down together at the kitchen table. In our household at least, any meaningful discussions tend to take place around our kitchen table.

My mind was buzzing as I laid out my lists, hoping that I had all the details Mike needed for an 'informed decision' to be made. But my nerve was wavering at the enormity of the responsibility I was about to take on.

Mike played devil's advocate, a role he took on with some relish, and fired off a series of questions.

'Supposing you have a flare-up of colitis, how will you cope with the horse?', 'What happens if we want to go away on holiday?' and 'What about unexpected expenses?' to name but a few.

I had most of these options covered as the livery was flexible. I would do as much of the work as I could, and if we were away on holiday or I was too ill to manage, I could pay extra to have the horse on full livery, where the yard staff would take over in my absence.

What didn't hold up to scrutiny was the budget. It was a close call… the bad news being that the balance sheet didn't quite add up. Income did not equal outgoings and an initial injection of cash was needed to start the ball rolling.

The good news was that I had a savings fund. Ever since my early twenties I had lusted after a Mercedes. A nice sporty little number – you know the one: two-door coupé with leather seats, walnut dashboard and all the trimmings, with that little circular symbol of success and independence standing proud on the bonnet, staring back at me every time I switched on the ignition. Over time, I had ferreted away small amounts of money and my fund had grown steadily for this, my one and only indulgence.

As Mike and I worked out the sums, I realised, with some regret, that the 'Mercedes fund' would have to be plundered in order to support the additional expense of buying a horse and augmenting her wardrobe. In view of this latest development, Mike saw his path to success in winning the argument against this foolhardy purchase. He pressed home his advantage.

'Well, you can kiss goodbye to your Mercedes if you buy this horse. You know that, don't you?' he cautioned, with just a hint of complacency creeping into his voice.

Visions of the sparkling paintwork on my two-door CLK started to fade into the distance and my resolve to purchase the horse suffered its first setback. Sensing that victory just might be at hand, Mike adjourned the meeting to allow me more time to ponder his words.

That was Mike's strength, his quiet deliberation. If he could, he always played for time, and he might have won, but for those chilling words: 'She's gone back to the dealers,' which greeted me the following day on my arrival at the riding school.

You see, Monday was a rest day for the horses following the weekend rush and there were no lessons. It was the only day of the week that staff were free to transport horses which needed to be moved. And Ballista had outstayed her welcome. She was eating without earning and wasn't a quick sale. In the business world no one needed a liability like Ballista.

I went home in turmoil and Mike's relieved, 'Well, that's the end of that then,' fell on deaf ears. I knew it was folly, but for all Mike's logic, something deep inside told me I had to have her. Believe me, I tried to be rational, tried to forget all about this feckless proposition; but at night, instead of the comforting oblivion of sleep, I spent the dark hours fighting an imagination fuelled by the pages of *Black Beauty* childhood reading and trying to put gruesome scenes of knackers' yards out of my mind.

In times of trouble there's only one place for me to go – to my mum. She is the one who has shared all my hopes, my exploits, my dreams, my triumphs and my failures. She is the one who has listened, tutted, been my conscience, doled out advice (even when it wasn't asked for), rolled up her sleeves when necessary and pitched her lot in with mine. There is nothing

I can't discuss with her and nothing I wouldn't share with her. I jumped into the car and drove straight round to my mum's house.

'What's the matter, dear?' she said as soon as she opened the front door.

She can always tell when trouble's brewing. Apparently, she says, it is written on my face.

Out poured my story, the pros and the cons, the responsibility, the step into the unknown.

'Oh, but you've always loved horses,' she exclaimed. 'Right from when you were a little girl; it was your childhood dream to own one.'

When I woke up the following morning, my head was no longer cluttered with ifs and buts and maybes. I had reached a crossroads in my life. This was no longer about the rights and wrongs of a decision; it was about throwing all the dice up into the air, taking a chance and seeing it through. My intuition told me that if I didn't grab this opportunity to try the one thing I'd always dreamed of, then I would dream on forever. With a clarity of vision that had hitherto escaped me, I got straight out of bed, picked up the phone and dialled the school.

'Get her back, I'll buy her,' I said softly into the mouthpiece.

Benz's cold, hard metal had just been replaced with the warm softness of flesh and blood.

CHAPTER 5

It was a cold, damp All Saints' Day afternoon and getting darker by the minute as I waited in my car at the riding school. The horsebox was late, and I cast my eye over the plastic bag of cash that lay on the front passenger seat beside me. I had picked up the money the previous day from my local bank.

'How would you like it?' the cashier had asked in a monotone.

'Um, as it comes, I suppose,' I replied.

The only noise was the hum of the bank counting machine and the rustle of notes.

'I'm buying a horse,' I blurted out unasked.

The cashier looked at me nonplussed and carried on counting out the cash. The bundles were checked and rechecked, together with my various forms of ID and proof of residence. Boxes were ticked on order forms, authorisation dockets were initialled and when everyone was finally satisfied that the transaction was in order, I stuffed the notes nervously into my shoulder bag, like a thief in the night, and ran back to my car as quickly as I could.

I looked up as lights appeared down the lane, and seconds later a horse trailer drew slowly to a halt outside the gates. My heart was thumping as the gates opened and the Land Rover pulled in beside me with its precious cargo. I jumped out of my car and the wind lashed my face as the Land Rover's engine was switched off and the lights were killed. The driver climbed out, gave me a nod and walked round to the trailer at the back. The doors were unlocked, the ramp came down and out flew my mare, like a ghostly, white silhouette in the gathering dusk, with her head held high, nostrils flaring and her mane and tail billowing in the wind.

That's how I'll always remember her, as she was on that first night: wild and fiery and proud. She came to me with nothing, no passport or paperwork, only the beauty God had given her, the vices man had taught her and the rope around her neck.

I stretched out my hand in the darkness and tried to stroke her neck, to calm her and give her some reassurance, but she twisted away from my touch. Her hooves clattered on the concrete yard as she pivoted up and down, trying to look around and adjust to her new surroundings. I heard one of the riding school horses snort in the background.

'Grab a headcollar...' someone shouted.

I ran to the tack room for a headcollar.

'...And she'll need a rug for the time being... Take one from Dusty's stable, he's about the same size as her.'

A rug appeared and was quickly put over her. It wasn't a bad fit, and she was declared ready for bed.

'Let her settle for the night.'

We took her to a stable which had been prepared earlier. It was one in a row that was situated round the back of the yard, where the livery horses were kept, away from the prying fingers of well-meaning children and the bustle of the riding school area. The mare didn't know it, but her status at the school had just gone up a notch, from working girl to privately owned and all the perks that went with it.

Knowing so little about horses, I decided from that day on that I would try to see the world through my horse's eyes, to look at things from her perspective, to try to understand why she reacts as she does. And maybe, in understanding her, I could learn more about myself in the process. Inevitably there are always two sides to a story, and this was her story as well as mine.

As I drove away from the yard, I felt the heavy weight of responsibility wrap itself around me like a cloak. I was all she had; it was up to me now to provide for her health, her well-being, her needs and her happiness.

But another feeling also crept over me as I drove home that night. I was ecstatic. I could barely contain myself as excitement welled up inside me and all my reservations vanished in a haze of euphoria.

Astoundingly, against all the odds, I had become a horse owner. Like Alice stepping through the looking glass, I had unwittingly been propelled into a different world, a world I had previously been unaware of. A section of society where priorities were turned upside down in favour of horses, where the bonds formed between fellow owners were instantaneous and where non-horse owners were left mystified by hours of horsey chit-chat that might just as well have been in a foreign language for all that they understood of it.

I went to bed that evening and had the best night's sleep I'd had in a fortnight.

CHAPTER 6

It is difficult to describe my feelings that morning, when I woke up to find myself 'with horse' so to speak; a bit like being with child, I suppose, especially for someone like me who'd never had any children. Reality had taken on a dreamlike quality. Was it all true? Had I really just bought a horse?

I was up and dressed in no time and barely stopped to eat breakfast before rushing off to the yard. I tried to stem my enthusiasm when I arrived, but couldn't quite manage the air of aplomb that the regulars seemed to possess. Making a beeline for my horse's stable, I leant over the door crooning, 'Hello, baby,' but her concentration on her morning hay never faltered. I don't know what I was expecting from the poor animal, maybe some small glimmer of recognition or even a welcoming whinny, but despite my attempts to evince a response, she never batted an eyelid. She remained stoical in the face of my nonsensical ramblings and utterly indifferent to the fact that she now had a new owner.

Buying a horse is a tricky business, where even the most experienced owners can make a mistake and the caveat of 'buyer beware' is never more pertinent. Generally, dealers are unlikely to know the full history of the horses they are selling, particularly if they have bought them from a market or another dealer. Sometimes, if the horse is properly documented, you may be able to contact the previous owner to learn a few details about their life elsewhere, but you are rarely given the whole story.

When I bought this mare she had no passport, and I was told that her paperwork had somehow been lost in transit. She was estimated to be 12 years old, and it was rumoured that she had been shipped from Holland to a UK horse-trader who had sold her to another dealer in Kent. The horse had then been placed temporarily at the riding school, where a prospective purchaser had expressed an interest. It was at this point in Ballista's life that I came on the scene, and when the original purchaser decided not to proceed, the ball was tossed into my court.

So it is hardly surprising that my horse remained tight-lipped while she assessed her situation, reserving judgement pending the new developments in her life. For the time being, at least, things weren't looking too bad: she had a nice stable with a deep, soft bed and lots of hay.

I took solace from the assurances of more experienced horse owners, who all declared, 'She'll get to know you in time. It's early days yet.'

The horse in the stable next-door-but-one to mine always whinnied when its owner came round the corner. Just hearing her footfall would set it off. How I longed to hear that same whinny from mine, the first indication of a fledgling bond between us. But I knew it was unrealistic and it made me think about my expectations; the product of a world where instant gratification is considered to be our due reward, no matter how shallow that response may be.

Horses are great levellers; offering no 'please' or 'thank you', they bring their owners down to earth with a jolt. They have no ego, just their natural instincts – a blueprint for survival handed down through generations of ancestors, whose very existence depended on this tried and tested set of inherited behavioural patterns.

By contrast, it seemed to me that humans had lost that connection between nature and their own psyche, confusing worth with the size of their bank balance or the number of material possessions they owned. And I suddenly realised that a reliance on superficiality creates a false sense of security, which soon crumbles when the fabric is tested.

Perhaps that is why so many of us are subconsciously searching for alternatives to fill an emotional void in our lives, and perhaps that was why I had felt so elated the previous evening.

As that first day progressed, I was amazed at how willing the horsey clan were to share their knowledge and experience with a 'first-timer'. Suddenly I knew the names of people I had seen around the yard for ages but had never spoken to; they became friends instead of just faces and a whole new social scene opened up for me. I am truly indebted to every single person who gave me their advice or proffered their opinion on every aspect of horse care. And that advice came thick and fast over the first few months, with my new learning curve taking on all the properties of a vertical ascent.

Borrowing a headcollar, I tentatively pushed back the bolt on the stable door and slipped in beside my new horse. For a second, she looked at me and I looked at her, as if we were weighing each other up like adversaries before the onset of battle. Brushing my nerves aside, I stepped forward and cautiously slipped the halter over her head, but fastening the buckle wasn't so easy. Horses aren't inanimate objects; they shake their heads and twist round to look at things. It took two fumbled attempts before I was ready to lead Ballista out of the stable.

Having cleared our first hurdle, I was shown how to tie up a horse safely on the yard, by attaching the lead rope to a piece of twine looped through a metal ring secured to the wall..

'Why can't I just tie her rope to the metal ring?' I queried.

'In case something startles her and she pulls back suddenly,' they said. 'Then the twine will break and the horse can move away from whatever frightened her. If she panics and can't get free, she could injure herself.'

'Right!' I said, trying to imagine myself with the mindset of an animal that uses 'flight' to escape from danger.

My next task was the grooming routine, starting from the ground and working my way up. I began by lifting up the feet to see if there were any stones or muck stuck in the grooves and cleaning them with a hoof pick. This looks like a simple task, but horses' feet are heavy; especially when they have ascertained you are a fair replacement for the foot you are holding and use you as a support. Removing the mud caked in the crevices isn't so easy either; it dries solid, not unlike concrete I mused to myself, as I struggled with the unfamiliar implement and the weight of the horse as she leant into me.

Moving higher up, all eyes were on me as I borrowed some brushes from the riding school. Advice and explanations peppered the yard.

'Don't kneel down to brush the lower leg. It's dangerous. You won't be able to get out of her way in time. She'll send you flying if something startles her. If you bend over at the waist, you'll be able to jump out of the way if anything happens.'

'I wouldn't stand directly behind her, especially when you're grooming her tail. Some horses are sensitive to movement behind them and might kick out. You're better off standing to one side; you're out of the firing line and she's less likely to score a direct hit.'

'You'll need to register ownership of that mare and she'll need a passport. New rules you know.'

No, I didn't, but then there wasn't much that I did know.

My new horse was apparently called Ballista. I didn't know who had chosen the name or where it had come from, but I hated it. In my opinion it was no name for either man or beast, and a pretty little mare like her definitely deserved something better. I decided that the question of a new name for Ballista was important enough to necessitate a period of cogitation, and I would have to confer with my other half in order to choose something more appropriate. I decided not to mention to Mike that, on occasion, I had also heard the word 'ballistic' bandied about. Could that reference to a rocket be a warning, a portent of things to come? It should have rung little alarm bells and led me to at least pose the question 'Why?', but I was besotted and my judgement duly clouded. I was blissfully unaware of the difficulties that lay ahead, and even if I'd known, I would probably have ploughed on regardless anyway. Put it down to age, I was pushing 50 by then – this was my dream and she was my girl.

Maybe it had something to do with the fact that I never had a family. I had moved along quite nicely in life, happy with my child-free lot, proud of my uncluttered home, quiet garden and baby-seat-free car. Occasionally I wondered whether or not I should do anything about starting a family, but the maternal instinct never made it out of the bag long enough for me to make up my mind. Nonetheless, we women ignore the ticking clock at our peril, and just when we think we are home free – bang goes a fuse. Suddenly, this dormant pile of hormones, impervious to offspring for all our childbearing years, explodes into life at the onset of menopause and latches on to the nearest equivalent. In my case, that happened to be a horse.

Back on the yard, I pondered my next question. Now that she was groomed and ready to ride, I needed to discuss the issue of a saddle and bridle for my new horse.

Simple, I thought, just like buying a dog's lead and collar – small, medium or large?

That gave everyone at the school a laugh. In fact, there was to be quite a lot of chuckling going on between 'those in the know' as I struggled with my ignorance.

'She has to be *fitted* for a saddle.'

'Does she? Why is that then?'

There is no such thing as a one-size-fits-all in the horsey world. Horses come in all shapes and sizes, thin ones, fat ones, wide ones and bony ones, short backs, long backs, broad backs and the rest. Saddles are the most important piece of kit for both horse and rider. Comfort and a perfect fit are absolutely essential. The rider's weight needs to be evenly spread across the horse's back, the saddle should sit in the centre of the horse's back and the 'line' of the saddle flap should be behind its shoulders to allow free movement. An ill-fitting saddle can rub, pinch, cause sores and any number of back problems. Horses only have their body language to tell us if something is wrong, and if they have something uncomfortable on their back they usually respond by trying to remove it. Unfortunately, this often means that their riders are the first to be rudely dumped on the ground.

In addition, there are a variety of saddle cloths and pads that are used underneath the saddle, although none of these will compensate for a saddle that has been badly fitted. Just to complicate matters further, we then have to throw in a human being and find something that is comfy for the rider to sit on too.

So, following a recommendation, I booked a reputable saddler to come and 'fit' my horse, and in the meantime there was some serious horsey shopping to be tackled. It was time to consult the essential items list that I had compiled the previous week.

CHAPTER 7

Sorting out some documentation for Ballista was another priority and I braced myself for a run-in with red tape. However, I was in for a pleasant surprise. After making a couple of enquiries, the whole process turned out to be relatively straightforward, and a few days later our postman came striding up the driveway with the passport application forms hot in his hand.

I ripped open the envelope, cleared a space on the kitchen table and carefully laid out the papers in a prominent position. This, I reasoned, would act as a gentle reminder to fill in the blanks and return the application in the envelope provided. All I had to contend with now was the minor matter of choosing a new name for the horse.

'What's in a name?' you might ask. Apparently quite a lot, if you believe the various articles and books that popped up during my research. According to the experts, no 'naming' should be undertaken lightly so I enlisted a willing posse of family and friends who rallied to the cause. Books of baby names were flushed from their forgotten hiding places, dusted off and pored over with just as much fervour as someone expecting their first child.

Mike became my sounding board as we tried all sorts of names and I would call them out to him as he worked in the office we had set up in our spare room. We thought of Sunday (the day I decided to buy her), but that would inevitably be shortened to Sun – too much like 'son' for me and this was my little girl we were talking about. Vanilla was another offering, as she was mostly white, but I decided that would probably be shortened to Van…?! And so it went on. Initially the replies were helpful and came with a selection of alternatives; sometimes just a variation of the original and sometimes a completely different offering. However, I gradually noticed that Mike's counter-suggestions became less frequent and the replies more lacklustre as the day wore on, until in the end, most of the names just met with a stony silence.

I fell back on my erstwhile sidekick, my mum, who had always been my first port of call before her position had been usurped by Mike. The telephone lines between her house and mine burned with more vigour over the next few days than they had over the past six months, until even the common niceties of telephonic communications were dispensed with.

Brrring! I pick up.

'Crystal,' my mum says.

'Naa,' I respond, and bang… down goes the handset.

I scoured the internet for horse names, until the frustratingly slow pace of our broadband connection nearly sent me bonkers. I checked out famous names, obscure names and Arabic names (the general consensus was that there were definitely some Arab genes floating around in her), but nothing seemed to fit. I even found myself wandering around WH Smith's, picking up the latest hotshot novels just to see what in-vogue names they were using for their heroines. But still those boxes on the Pet ID registration form remained stubbornly blank, mocking my indecision every time I sat down at the kitchen table.

To take my mind off it I returned to my shopping list, and with Mike in tow, I headed out for some serious horsey shopping, which turned out to be an education in itself. Equestrian shops tend to come in two types: the smaller ones, which look like they're bursting at the seams with tempting displays of saddles, tack, accessories, rugs, clothing and merchandise all squeezed into a host of nooks and crannies; and then there are the larger retailers. These bastions of equestrian goods are housed in huge warehouses, large enough to host a fleet of aircraft. Their cavernous depths swallow you up as you wander around the endless racks of stock, intoxicated by the heady smells of new leather and herbal horsey treats that hang in the air like a veritable smog.

The problem with 'choice' is universal to all ardent shoppers. You know you have a budget, but as soon as you enter the premises you see all the 'smart' gear, colour coordinated with matching extras that catch your eye at every turn. Some of the items are absolute necessities, some you think you might need later on, some you're not sure about and others you know you don't need at all, but you're determined to buy anyway.

I caressed the bridles suspended on pegs along the wall, stroked the saddles, compared softness and design, looked at the various styles of stirrups and wondered about girths. Moving on, I tested the grooming equipment; did the brushes fit neatly into my hand, were the bristles too stiff or too soft, were they durable? I went in search of a first aid box, scissors, shampoo, sterile dressings, ointments and creams. Having bought most of the equipment on my essentials list, I then spent ages agonising over which rugs to buy – checking out the different materials, padding and breathability. Finally, with Mike yawning in the background, I made my choice, buying a combination of seasonal rugs and a couple of neck covers, with the proviso that I could return them if they didn't fit properly.

'That's no problem,' the assistant said. 'But you must make sure that the rugs are kept clean if you want to bring them back, otherwise we can't accept them.'

'Oh, I'll bring them back immediately if they don't fit,' I said, missing the point entirely.

'Well, what I mean is, don't put the new rugs directly onto the horse without something else on its back – like a blanket or another rug, to stop any hairs sticking to the new rug.'

Now I understood. White horse, dark rug, lots of hairs. Yes, I could see that might just be a problem if I wanted to bring the rugs back…

We flung the shopping into the car, and on my way back to the yard I decided to make a quick pit stop at our house. My first priority was to drop Mike off; I could tell from the monosyllabic grunts that came my way as I chatted, that he was in serious danger of becoming comatose through boredom. Secondly I needed to pick up some sort of protective overall for the horse.

Mike gave a sigh of relief as he opened the front door, and I dashed in behind him, making a beeline for the airing cupboard.

'Now what're you after?' he asked, puzzled.

'I'm looking for one of our old cotton sheets,' I said, rummaging through a stack of bed linen. 'I'm gonna use that to put over Ballista's back while I try the rugs on.'

'Hmm… that's not a bad idea,' Mike concurred, becoming more communicative now that he was once again in the familiar embrace of the arms of his computer chair.

I found what I was looking for at the bottom of the pile, and two minutes later I was in the car, heading down the driveway.

At the riding school everyone checked out the shopping while I led my horse out and proudly popped on her first rug.

Standing back to admire my purchase, I said, 'How's that then?'

A diplomatic silence.

'It doesn't fit.'

'Doesn't fit? It covers her back and her sides, what do you mean it doesn't fit?'

Then the dissection took place.

Someone pulled at the neckline. 'Look at this. It's too big,' they said, lifting the rug away from the neck by about twelve inches.

'And the back is too long – that seam should be just about level with the top of the tail, not hanging down over the tail, like that.'

Crestfallen, I knew there was no alternative. I would have to take the rugs back and buy either a smaller size or a different make of rug, more suited to a slim horse with narrow shoulders. I telephoned Mike, who was unimpressed. He hates shopping at the best of times, and whilst the novelty of a horsey shop had appealed as a one-off, I suspected that his interest sprang more from a desire to exercise a cost-limitation influence over me rather than any real input towards the more emotionally driven aspects of the shopping itself.

Second time around I took my best friend Lorna with me, a much more enthusiastic companion, who really knows how to do justice to shopping, even if it's only the window kind. Better still, I could hide my ignorance behind Lorna, who knew even less about horses than I did. She was totally unabashed about asking the saleswomen all manner of seemingly silly questions.

Faced with a dazzling array of unfamiliar objects, she ploughed on, undaunted, 'So, what are these things for?' and 'Why are these straps like this?' and 'Well I never!' whilst I stood behind, shrugging my shoulders and raising my eyebrows at the sales staff in an apologetic way. At the same time I listened intently to all the answers and stored away as much information as I could.

Lorna was also adept at getting good value for money.

'Look at this one over here,' she'd call out. 'I know it's £15 more, but feel the quality in that!'

There was another rather sneaky reason for asking Lorna to come with me on 'the shop' instead of Mike. It gave me the option of being, shall we say, economical with the truth if he decided to delve too deeply into the numerics of the latest shopping trip and the extent of the additional finances required.

With the shop floor virtually carpeted by an assortment of horse rugs, we finally made a decision. I exchanged the rugs I'd bought previously, paid the difference, (funny how you never seem to come out with anything that was cheaper than your original purchase), loaded up the car again and off we went.

It was on our way home that the impasse over the horse's new name was finally broken. I was driving along the dual carriageway, when whoosh… I was overtaken by the most beautiful Mercedes coupé, all rich blue coach-work, sleek lines and sparkling alloys. Whoa, I thought to myself a little wistfully, I'll never own one of those now.

And then it came to me. Mercedes. MERCEDES! That's IT! I rolled the name around my tongue and tested it out loud, causing Lorna's head to jerk upwards from her chest, where it had lolled earlier when a snooze got the better of her.

She blinked, trying to focus. 'What was that? Did you say something?'

'Mercedes, Lorn. That's what I'll call my girl; she's beautiful, with sleek lines, a Mercedes of the horse world.'

'But you won't call her Mercedes all the time, will you? It's bound to be shortened to something else, so what would you shorten it to?' Lorna interjected.

I paused for only a second, 'Mercedes will be her official name and I'll call her "Sadie" for short.'

So that was that; I could finally lay that inscrutable blank form to rest and pop it in the post, where it would mock me no more.

Needless to say the day finally ended with a boot full of gear, two satisfied shopaholics, a reasonably happy horse whose rugs now fitted and an entente cordiale at home.

CHAPTER 8

With my finances still reeling from the shopping trip it was now the turn of the saddler to take a cut. There really is no substitute for these equine tailors and a good one is as sought after as a gentleman's outfitter from Savile Row. I won't bore you with the various types of saddle it is possible to purchase, suffice to say that information overload kicked in less than half an hour into our session. It is possible to pick up a cheap saddle for around £500, but on average you can double that price and, for those with deep pockets, bespoke or competition saddles can cost thousands. As my budget was under scrutiny, I eventually chose a brown, middle-of-the-range saddle and was surprised to see it handed over without any stirrups.

'No stirrups?' I enquired.

'We're coming to those,' was the droll response. 'That's just the cost of the saddle.'

I soon discovered that stirrup leathers and stirrups are bought separately, and the cost depends on the style of stirrup and quality of leather.

Of course, silly me! Why should I automatically presume that the purchase of a saddle included the stirrups?

The saddle fitter continued, 'I expect you'll be needing a girth as well then, if this is the first time you are purchasing tack?'

'Yes, yes, I'll need a girth as well,' I said, wondering how else I was supposed to keep the saddle on the horse's back without a girth.

As for the bridle, yes, you've guessed it, that's another minefield. The purchase of this 'headset' does not include a 'bit' for the horse's mouth or any reins for the rider, which are usually purchased separately. The variation of bits alone is mind-boggling to a novice, and again the technicalities of most of them went straight over my head. In fact, because of the plethora of shapes and sizes on the market, some shops have what are called 'bit banks', where you can purchase or borrow different bits until you find one that both horse and rider are happy with. After the usual deliberations, I decided on a 'snaffle' bit which is a common one used for non-problematic horses. I reasoned that I could always buy another one later, if Sadie needed something more severe.

Next up were the fancy accessories. For the more pampered horse the 'common or garden' leather browbands can be quickly replaced with much more eye-catching varieties such as a chain link, coloured ribbon, velvet or even dazzling diamanté ones. I have to admit to being tempted, particularly by the diamanté browbands that sparkled as they caught the sunlight, but at this juncture, I decided that I was definitely sticking to the cheap and cheerful.

Having purchased all this stiff new leather tack, I had been advised to soak it all with a good proprietary brand of saddle soap or balm to nourish the leather and keep it in good condition. I decided to tackle this little task at home, where I could take my time over it, sitting in comfort, watching TV. I meticulously undid all the straps and buckles on my bridle to make sure I didn't miss an inch and when every piece had been polished and buffed to perfection, I was left with an assortment of leather straps in varying lengths and sizes, together with a metal bit, all laid out on newspaper on our living room floor. However, when it came to reassembling my brand new bridle, try as I might, I just couldn't figure it out.

In desperation I called out to Mike, 'Honey!'

But if I was expecting any inspiration from that quarter, I was soon disabused of this notion when Mike poked his head round the door, took one look and promptly disappeared, muttering, 'You've gotta be joking…'

In the end there was only one option. I swallowed my pride, threw all the pieces into a bag and took them back to the riding school to seek professional help.

CHAPTER 9

Of course, along with the new horse, I had to have a new car. Well, not quite new, second hand actually, a bit like the horse I suppose. As I said to Mike, the Ford had really seen better days with over 100,000 miles on the clock, and there was the question of boot space. There would be bags of feed and bales of bedding, boots, buckets and a whole host of other paraphernalia, all essential and all needing to be transported. But more importantly, the final weeks of autumn heralded a downturn in weather conditions and I would need a four-wheel drive to get me backwards and forwards to the horse with some degree of certainty.

When it rained, the narrow country roads leading to the riding school were often doused in slushy mud, brought down from the fields on the gigantic wheels of farm tractors and dumped haphazardly along the road, where it lay waiting to catch you out as you slammed on the brakes in the face of an oncoming vehicle. With winter fast approaching and the nights drawing in, the surrounding countryside would be rapidly transformed by the legacy of freezing temperatures. Soon the blades of grass on the roadside verges would be sculpted by the hoar frost and the hedgerows would shimmer with the gossamer threads of spiders' webs, decked with tiny droplets of icy water, hanging like diamonds from a necklace around nature's throat. I reminded Mike that there was also the likelihood of snow during those wintery months, which would slap a further layer of pristine, arctic beauty over the already perilous surface of those winding lanes.

In other years I had been free to tailor my visits according to the weather forecast, weighing up the likelihood of any dry or sunny days and picking the best of them for my lessons. If the weather took an unexpected turn for the worse there was always the option of changing my times or cancelling my lesson completely.

Now things were different. Now I had commitments. I needed to get to my girl whatever the weather, and only a four-wheel drive would do the job. Mike was on the internet in a flash, scouring the 'For Sale' advertisements for something suitable.

Back at the yard, I was now a regular, arriving on most days to spend an hour with my new horse and usually leaving two to three 'where-has-the-time-gone?' hours later. When I first bought Sadie, I imagined the freedom of just popping up to the yard, tacking up my horse and having a ride whenever I pleased, without having to phone for an appointment or fit my working hours around the availability of an instructor. And whilst this was still true to a certain extent, in reality things are never quite as straightforward as they first appear.

As a riding school client, it had never been necessary for me to be party to the tacking-up process. Usually when I arrived, my allocated horse was all groomed and ready, with its saddle and bridle firmly in place. Pre-horse ownership, the most I'd ever had to cope with was adjusting the length of the stirrups, and the majority of the time, even that was done for me. But everything was to change now that I had my own horse. Suddenly I became aware of all the little things I had never noticed before. There was the unerring ability of the riding school staff to tack up a horse in about three minutes flat; a task which seemed to take me ten times longer. Then there was the actual weight of the saddle itself, carrying it around and having the strength to lift it above shoulder height in order to place it gently onto the back of my horse. It wasn't until I had to do it myself, that I realised just how heavy those saddles were. And then another thought struck me – the number of times that I had seen riding school staff walking out of the tack room, casually wielding a saddle on each arm. Those women must have arms like girders of steel, and I marvelled at them with a new reverence…

Once I had the saddle on the horse, it then needed to go in exactly the right place. I would fumble around, adjusting it bit by bit, until it was so far back behind the withers (horse's shoulders) that I would have to take it off and reposition it again. The saddle cloth then needed to be 'lifted' in front to create air space between the horse and the cloth, without disturbing the saddle's position that I had spent so long perfecting. As soon as I was satisfied that everything could be strapped into place, a contest would ensue between me and Sadie, who would try to sabotage my attempts to secure the girth before the saddle slipped, by fidgeting or blowing out her tummy.

I discovered that there was definitely a knack to placing the bit into a horse's mouth (without having my fingers lacerated by a rather large set of gnashers) and slipping the bridle neatly over the top of the head in one fell swoop without squashing the ears into the shape of a concertina.

Finally, there were the 'brushing boots', which needed to be wrapped around the horse's lower leg, to protect against knocks and bruises. With a simple Velcro fastening, I thought, how can I go wrong? Quite easily apparently, as I blithely put the left boots onto the right legs and the right ones onto the left legs. Still, I consoled myself, at least I didn't put them on upside down.

Despite my ignorance, Sadie seemed to accept all this fumbling activity with inordinate grace. Over the next few months my technique gradually improved as I became more confident, and although there was still a squashed ear on occasion, Sadie never seemed to hold it against me.

Up to this point I had only ever ridden the horses at the riding school and had always been satisfied with the progress of my riding ability. However, riding school horses are the diamonds of the equine industry. They put up with an endless stream of beginners and novice riders, from kids to grown-ups, all running through the same boring sequences weekend after weekend with the occasional 'hack' in the countryside thrown in for good measure. At the same time, these good-natured horses are expected to put up with a cacophony of noises, ranging from excited children to lawn mowers, motorbikes, cars, aeroplanes and a variety of other man-made devices designed to make any normal horse bolt clean across the countryside. It is these special qualities and amenable temperaments that make a riding school horse worth its weight in gold, because anyone, from beginner to the more experienced rider, can come away feeling that they have achieved something from their ride.

In my naïvety I was blissfully unaware of these things, but I soon found out that there was a vast difference between having a lesson on a riding school horse and setting out alone, even if it was just practising in the school arena.

The teacher not only instructs the rider, acting as a mirror to correct their body position, but they also provide format and structure to the lessons. They tell you when to pick up trot, when to canter and what shapes to ride, so that the horse is worked equally on both its left and right sides. They can see in an instant if the horse is responding as it should, or whether the message from its rider has been lost in transmission.

But here I was, on the yard, in a cloud of blind ignorance, eagerly anticipating our first ride together, on our own. So, off we went to the indoor school, where I was to come face to face with my nemesis: that 'she's not a riding school horse…' comment, which had been echoing around in my head ever since I'd heard it.

Once inside the arena, I expected Sadie to walk on, automatically keeping to a neat line around the outside edge, just like all the other riding school horses do. But Sadie wasn't programmed like the riding school horses and she was smart too. She knew immediately that there was no 'Teacher' in the arena to get on her case if she misbehaved, and after a few faltering steps, she slowly came to a halt in the centre of the arena and stood there, motionless. I squeezed with my legs… nothing happened… I squeezed again, harder this time. Still Sadie stood there. Resolute. All of a sudden I was on my own and, inexorably, the tenuous lines of communication that existed between Sadie and me quickly broke down.

CHAPTER 10

As those first few weeks unfolded, I discovered that far from being a nice, quiet hack, Sadie was totally different to any other horse I had ridden.

Riding school horses are quite willing to help a novice out. They are used to interpreting a leg movement or command, even when they aren't as clear-cut as they should be. This wasn't so with Sadie, who refused to acknowledge any riding commands that weren't delivered correctly or with absolute conviction. If there was the merest hint of ambiguity, she ignored me, and the few times I did get it right we often had a difference of opinion.

Sadie was also insecure without the company of other horses and was reluctant to do anything on her own or go anywhere unfamiliar. She started at every leaf and shadow, some of which were real and some only imagined. But her worst nightmare were the tiny birds that burst from the hedgerows as they flew backwards and forwards, foraging for nesting materials. Sadie perceived these comings and goings as a personal assault and would shy violently to one side, her metal shoes scrabbling on the smooth tarmac as she struggled to keep her footing.

In fact, Sadie was only really happy with another horse's bottom in front of her nose, comfortable in the knowledge that any hidden danger would be ousted by the horse in front. This earned her the nickname of 'tail-end Charlie' because she always brought up the rear when we went out on a hack through the countryside.

But for all her fears, Sadie was also very intelligent; she found going into the arena boring and would make up her own fun as I tried to concentrate on my riding position or practise routine manoeuvres. Generally her modus operandi fell into one of two routines, which were then peppered with a repertoire of assorted tricks.

The first routine was quite straightforward: within the first ten seconds of entry into the arena she'd glide to a halt, plant her feet firmly in front of her and refuse to budge. Any attempt to make her go forward had the opposite effect and usually resulted in reverse gear. Then we would battle it out together along the lines of two steps forward, three steps back, until Sadie decided to bounce both front legs off the ground together to see how quickly I would lose my nerve. Unfortunately, my inexperience meant that I was no match for Sadie and she knew it; her naughtiness sapped my confidence and I was often close to tears by the end of a session together. But this was where my riding instructors stepped in with their much-needed advice, unfailing support and the occasional shoulder to cry on.

We tried a different approach. I decided to join one of the regular group lessons at the school in the hope that Sadie would be better behaved in the company of other horses. That way, I reasoned, I could improve both my riding ability and my confidence at the same time. However, I had reckoned without Sadie's contentious point of view, and this was where she changed tactics, substituting her previous routine with another, just as crafty, alternative.

On average there were usually four to five horses in every class. All the horses would enter the school together and form a line around the perimeter where everyone would follow-my-leader, Sadie included. So far, so good. The lesson would then proceed normally, without a hint of rebellion as Sadie bided her time, giving off an air of relaxed submission and lulling everyone into a false sense of security. We usually managed to get about halfway through a lesson unscathed, until whoosh... Sadie would hit the panic button. An inoffensive object, that Sadie had been happy to ride past for the last ten circuits, suddenly assumed horrific proportions and became a loathsome bête noir. It might be someone's jacket, a handbag, a jumping pole propped up in the corner or an unnoticed sweet wrapper, but whatever it was Sadie would twist to one side, dance on the spot and refuse to go forward, creating a knock-on effect that generally reduced the ride to mayhem.

After a few subtle and not-so-subtle suggestions from the instructors, it was decided that Sadie's behaviour was too disruptive for her to continue in the group lessons and that my best course of action would be private lessons tailored to our specific needs. By this time, I was beginning to think that I would never be able to ride Sadie. Often in those early months there were days when I dreaded the thought of having to ride her and I would tack her up with butterflies in my stomach, wondering what could possibly go wrong next. At other times, our lack of progress ground me into despondency and I would weep with sheer frustration. But I had set myself a goal and was dogged in my determination; I knew that one day I would put that saddle on Sadie with a new self-confidence born of hard work and perseverance.

Things were not all sweetness and light with our other recent purchase either. Having been tasked with replacing my ageing motor, Mike had done his research and snapped up a four-wheel-drive estate car.

'This is just perfect for you,' he enthused. 'It's got everything you need and you're gonna love it. I know you will.'

And I did… until my newly acquired doyen of motoring perfection, the 'one-to-replace-all-others', suffered a computer malfunction and, like a ghastly rerun of my morning ride with Sadie, refused to start – leaving me stranded in the supermarket car park. Frenzied calls to the roadside rescue company saw the car eventually carted off to a local garage. There it remained in situ, pending an electronics check in the morning, whilst I ended up riding shotgun in the front passenger seat of the breakdown truck, surrounded by umpteen bags of shopping.

When I eventually arrived home later that evening, I wailed to Mike in desperation, 'I've bought a horse I can't ride and a car I can't drive.'

Mike took a deep breath and slowly shook his head from side to side.

'Well, the car's easy enough to fix,' he said. 'But the horse… It looks like it's going to take a lot longer to fix her!'

I sat in stony silence, implacable.

'The fact is, I'm surrounded by irrational females, all acting on impulse,' he continued. 'The cat's bad enough…' referring to our homophobic rescue cat who takes fright at the sight of an overcoat but becomes a hissing tornado the minute any other feline has the temerity to put so much as a paw in our back garden, '…and now you've bought a bloomin' horse that's as nutty as a fruitcake. If you had to have a horse, why didn't you buy a gelding? Males are so much more grounded than females,' he grumbled rhetorically.

CHAPTER 11

The trigger that really made me reassess my approach to riding happened one day when Sadie was being particularly awkward. We had been riding for about five minutes in the indoor arena, warming up with a short walk and a few steps of trot, before moving on to circle the top end of the school. As we approached the corner, Sadie flatly refused to go near it, backing up every time I asked her to go forward. I was baffled. This corner was absolutely empty. There were no poles or boxes or any other items in it that she could possibly object to, yet she still refused to go forward. I gave her a sharp tap with my crop and, in response to this encouragement, she jumped back again, nothing too dramatic, just enough to make me lose my nerve. Sadie had quickly cottoned on to the fact that I was nervous of her and realised that the more she played up, the shorter our ride would be.

I heard one of the instructors coming into the school for a private lesson, and with one glance in our direction she summed up the whole scenario. Marching straight over, she grabbed Sadie's reins.

'You have got to get to grips with this horse. She's taking advantage of you and the more you let her get away with it, the worse it'll be,' she said sternly.

I took a long, hard look at myself and I knew she was right. It is always difficult to face up to the truth about ourselves, especially when we are found to be lacking in some respect; maybe we are not as talented or as knowledgeable as we think we are and we become defensive if anyone suggests otherwise. Subconscious pressure from our peers and the competitive world around us can make us feel that if we are anything less than perfect then, somehow, we have failed. We should be proud of our achievements, however humble; but until we own up to our shortcomings, we can't do anything about improving our situation.

I had been riding for about five years before I bought Sadie and thought I was quite a good rider. In reality I hadn't progressed much beyond beginners' level; I could try to fool myself, but sadly I couldn't fool Sadie. If I wanted to ride Sadie then I would have to master the ability and technique that was required; I would never be a world class horsewoman, nor did I want to be, but I did want to be the best that I could. There was nothing else for it; I had to go right back to basics, starting with private lessons on the lunge rein.

The idea with this type of lesson is that the riding instructor retains control over the horse by clipping a long lunge rope to the bridle. The horse then moves in a circle around the instructor, allowing the rider to concentrate on a good body position and the correct leg commands (or leg aids as they are more commonly known).

Back on the lunge and with Sadie safely under control, the instructor went one step further and removed my feet from the stirrups, so that I had to concentrate on my balance, keeping my bum firmly in the saddle. You see, when Sadie skedaddled off to one side, it wasn't my stirrups that were going to keep me in the saddle – it was the combination of balance, seat and legs that would stop me from falling off. This practice is much harder than it looks to the casual observer, and my muscles complained bitterly after these lessons. But it is great for building confidence, and the more secure I felt in the saddle, the more I was able to focus on dealing with Sadie when things were not going to plan.

All work and no play is a bad programme for anyone and both Sadie and I needed time out to enjoy each other. She loved to run free in the arenas where she felt safe, with no pressure to conform or follow anyone else's rules. And I loved to watch her; with nothing else to do other than enjoy her company. I would turn her loose in the indoor school where she would amble along until she found the perfect spot for a roll. Then she would turn in a tight circle and boof... down she'd go with a grunt, onto the ground, throwing all four legs in the air as she squirmed from side to side. When she'd finished, she'd hoist herself up onto her feet and shake herself down. The movement would start from her head and ripple back through her body, sending a great cloud of fine dust particles flying through the air. And then she'd spin round and canter off, throwing her head from side to side with her long, white tail streaming out behind her. Sometimes, when Sadie was going full pelt down the long side of the arena, she would skid to a halt in the corner, twist round quickly on her front legs and bounce her back legs up and down on the spot, like a pogo stick. At the same time, she would fling her head up high, snorting two hot streams of breath from her nostrils that condensed in the cold air like smoke from a steam train, which always brought a smile to my face. Sadie would lick her lips and look at me, I would wander over to stroke her neck and off she'd go again.

And as I sat at the side of the arena, lost in the flow of her graceful movements, I found myself engulfed by the timeless bonds that have existed throughout the ages between humans and horses; how man's survival seemed somehow intrinsically linked to the horse. I thought of previous generations who had relied on the horse for their livelihood, used them as a source of transport, valued them as a symbol of wealth and enjoyed them as a sporting challenge. Even today, with all the advances in modern technology, the horse still remains a key element in the lives of so many people and not just here in the Kent countryside, but worldwide. Then I remembered the darker side of mankind, his penchant for war, and my mind wandered back through history. From the early Crusades to the devastation wrought by the world wars in the 20th century, the horse had remained constant to man. Side by side in death, as in life, the courage and loyalty of those horses had triumphed over adversity, where everything man had asked for had been given.

Watching my horse in the quiet solitude of the arena, I felt my heart swell with pride and emotion. Through her I felt that connection with my ancestors, felt my feet firmly grounded in the same soil they had trod and I felt I had found my place in the world. She became my link to all the generations that had gone before me and made me feel part of the great continuation of life.

A few days later Sadie's new passport shot through our letterbox. As soon as I saw the envelope, big and square on the hallway mat, my heart skipped a beat. I ripped open the top end of the package and, sure enough, there it was – official verification that Sadie now belonged to me. I pulled out the document with its shiny plastic cover and fondled it lovingly; the printed name: Mercedes (Sadie) stared back at me through the white window in the blue cover. I read every page and checked every detail until I was satisfied that no mistakes or typing errors had been made, nor any minor detail missed, that could otherwise jeopardise the validity of such a precious record. And on the last but one page, marked Medicinal Treatment, I solemnly signed the declaration that excludes the animal definitively from slaughter for human consumption; banishing the chilling thought from my mind of all those declarations that went unsigned.

A new section had been added to the filing cabinet in Mike's office, between 'Guarantees' and 'Insurance', marked simply 'Horse'. It was already crammed with an assortment of paperwork and receipts, and I popped her passport in amongst the rest. Somehow her purchase seemed all the more real now that I had the document safely stashed away – proof positive she was mine.

CHAPTER 12

Mercedes wasn't the only new horse on the livery yard. A few weeks before her arrival, another first-time horse owner, Donna, had bought a beautiful, big, black mare who now occupied the stable directly opposite Sadie. The two horses were the antithesis of each other. Donna's horse was as black as night, built like a tank and level-headed, with a calm, trustworthy temperament. She was called Nobelle, and it suited her; she was a leader amongst mares. When a group of horses are turned out together in a field, they quickly form a 'pecking order' of dominance between themselves and Nobelle soon became established as the head of the herd.

In contrast to Nobelle, Sadie was a fragile mare; slender-legged with big, bony knees. She lacked confidence on her own and saw demons hiding in every corner. Maybe it was Nobelle's strength and dependability that drew Sadie to her, because they soon established a horsey rapport over the doors of their stables and spent many a quiet day grazing together in the large livery field. Sadie loved Nobelle and wherever Nobelle went, Sadie would go too. Nobelle was so amenable with horses and humans alike that I often took advantage of this friendship to coerce Sadie into a course of action that would otherwise have been unachievable on my own. I learnt that brute strength was never enough to persuade a horse to do something; you had to be a lot more cunning than that.

Donna and I became firm friends; it was reassuring to have another first-time owner on the yard, someone to chat to and exchange ideas with. We had lots of fun comparing notes on a multitude of equine topics ranging from grooming techniques to types of feed and preferred flavours of horsey treats. When we were at the yard together, we would bring our mares out of their stables and tie them side by side so that we could have a natter while we groomed. There would be Donna and me, bent double, cleaning feet, oiling hooves, trimming legs and washing tails, chatting away ten to the dozen about the idiosyncrasies of horsey behaviour, whilst time evaporated into thin air. Sometimes we would go out on a leisurely hack through the countryside together, because Sadie always behaved herself – or nearly always – when we were out with Nobelle. I knew that with Nobelle in front and Sadie's nose tucked firmly in behind that great black bottom all of her demons would be banished and we could enjoy our ride together.

It was only when we were back on the yard that, suddenly, one of us would remember forgotten tasks, or a husband or two, notice the time and gasp, 'Goodness me! Is that the time? Gonna have to rush now.'

These words always precipitated a frenzy of activity, sweeping up and packing away, culminating in the thud of car doors as we beat a hasty retreat to our respective homes.

Later in the evening, over a glass of wine or two, Mike would often ask, 'What have you been up to today?'

'I've been horse riding with Donna, honey,' I'd reply.

To which he'd laugh and say, 'Horse riding? You two spend most of your time horse chatting, if you ask me. It's a wonder there's any time left for riding!'

It was around this time that I started to notice a rather curious phenom-enon; I seemed to be more forgetful of late. These memory lapses appeared to be directly related to the amount of time I spent with Sadie, and I seemed to lose the ability to multitask in all but horsey-related matters. This, my friends assured me, was a positive sign; some parts of the brain were obviously fully functional, meaning we could probably rule out early-onset Alzheimer's.

Nonetheless, in an attempt to rectify this aberration I would compile a list of all those little innocuous things that needed to be done on a specific day, such as post a letter, pick up some bread, collect Mike's trousers from the dry cleaners, etc. and stick it to the dashboard. I would then drive over to Sadie, safe in the knowledge that everything was neatly written down and completely under control. The afternoon would waft by in peace and harmony until a mad dash home through rush hour traffic would see me sitting on our driveway minus the bread for the following morning's breakfast, letter still in my handbag and Mike's trousers still firmly under lock and key at the dry cleaners. Yikes, what a brain!

One evening when I was promising faithfully to remember tomorrow the task I had forgotten today, Mike smiled ruefully and said, 'Sometimes I think you love that horse more than you love me.'

'Don't be daft, darling,' I said, saddened by the hint of seriousness behind the jocularity. 'Of course I don't love her more than you. I love her in a different way, that's all. It's like any relationship. What about me and my mum?'

'What about you and your mum?' Mike said, mystified.

'I love her too, but not in the same way that I love you.'

'I should hope not!' spluttered Mike.

'But that's the point, and it's the same with Sadie. I know that you think I put her first. Well, maybe I do sometimes, but that's because she's vulnerable and totally dependent on me. She's like a child to me. I would never have gone ahead with the purchase if I wasn't prepared to take on that commitment. You can make yourself a sandwich if your dinner is late, but she can't. In fact, you make yourself a sandwich even when your dinner's isn't late, just 'cause you're feeling a bit peckish,' I said, emphasising the point by prodding my finger into the spongy recesses of Mike's tummy.

I needed to make sure that Mike understood what I was driving at, so I continued, 'Do you remember when we sat at this table and discussed buying her and I told you I couldn't do it without your support? I knew that you weren't keen on the idea of me buying a horse, but the fact that you supported me despite your reservations meant a lot to me – even more so now that Sadie has become such a big part of my life.'

'My reservations,' Mike said, 'were mainly centred on the fact that I didn't think you really understood how much time, effort and money were involved in owning a horse. I don't like to see you rushing around, trying to fit everything in. I honestly thought you would be better off just having riding lessons.'

'No one can really know what is best for someone else,' I said. 'Half the time we don't know ourselves, until we experience it. But that's the whole point. You *did* support me, despite your misgivings; you made all this possible for me and I really appreciate that. Having Sadie is such a wonderful experience; she's given me a different perspective on life and I've learnt so much from her.'

'I've learnt something as well,' Mike said, as he tapped the side of my head with his fingers. 'Inside there, is a horsey brain. The subject only needs to flit across your mind and you become instantly transformed; like a form of hypnotic autosuggestion, you're programmed to forget everything else the minute someone mentions anything to do with horses. We need to install an "off" button to switch you from "horse mode" to "normal" every now and again.'

I decided not to upset Mike further by observing that, lately, horse mode and normal had seemingly merged into one. We just enjoyed the moment, and our laughter, as he wrapped his big arms around me and squeezed me tight.

CHAPTER 13

I don't know what possessed me to do it, maybe some vague notion that if I took part, it would be something to aim for; I'm not sure, but I went ahead anyway. In the run up to Christmas most businesses lay on some form of jollity to celebrate the festive season and our yard was no exception – but their idea of a 'jolly' was a Christmas jumping show. The jumps were tiny, most of them less than a foot off the ground, so that all ages and abilities could take part in the fun and everyone who managed to get over the jumps without a refusal or knocking down a pole would be presented with a 'clear round' rosette. I had never taken part in anything like this before and became carried away with the notion that now I had my own horse we could take part in a show and maybe even walk away with a rosette! The poles were so low that Sadie could walk over them if she wanted to, but I was aiming for a steady trot that would see us over them in relative comfort. Who was I trying to kid…?

The day of the long-awaited Christmas jump-off arrived and I turned up at the riding school, feeling a strange mix of excitement tinged with apprehension. As soon as I had parked the car I went over to the indoor arena to check out the 'course', poked my head over the top of the door and gasped.

I'd been duped! No one at the school had mentioned the Christmas decorations. Whilst the jumps had been set up as I expected, with about eight mini jumps including a small 'triple' jump (where the horse pops over three poles in quick succession), every item was festooned with fronds of tinsel that danced and shimmered beneath the beams of the overhead lighting. Multicoloured foil was wrapped around the cross poles like winking snakes writhing on a branch, and potted shrubs, holly and a miniature plastic

Christmas tree peppered the arena like sentries, displaying the number and sequence of each jump. Then there were those wretched coloured balloons that lay silently by the gateway, deceptively motionless, just waiting for a wisp of wind to bring them to life, like crouching predators biding their time. The girls had done a great job setting out the course, it all looked so professional – but my heart sank, and I knew that whatever Sadie's brain was wired up to would blow a fuse when it saw this lot.

I adjourned to the tack room with a heavy heart and considered withdrawing from the jump-off.

'But why?' I knew they would all ask, and then I would have to admit my fears and lose face. No, I couldn't do that... and let Sadie win? What was I thinking of?

I grabbed my saddle with new conviction – I had been making steady progress on Sadie over the last few weeks – I would just take things slowly. We'd be fine, I convinced myself; after all, the show must go on...

All the competitors had their order of entry, and the outdoor arena was set up with a small cross pole in the centre, so that riders could have a practice warm-up before their number was called for the main event. We did a few circuits and then my name was called.

'They're ready for you, Gillian.'

A huddle of spectators parted as we entered the indoor school, and poor Sadie's eyes nearly popped out of her head at the spectacle of jumps which lay before her. This is where I should have taken charge and ridden forward with confidence; but then, I suppose, that is what learning to ride is all about. To my shame, I forgot everything that my instructor had previously told me. Sadie immediately sensed my lack of conviction and from that moment on I was lost.

We did a half-hearted trot over the first pole, before Sadie put the brakes on and flatly refused to go over the next pole. Reinforcements were at hand and one of the girls promptly came over to shoo Sadie forward from behind, which worked, after a fashion, and she did a funny half-hop over the second jump. But the third cross pole just wasn't in the frame and, on the approach, Sadie downed tools all together. She pranced on the spot, weaved to the side to go round it and then reversed five steps back. I was totally out of my depth. I thought, I'll just have to get off, and I slipped my feet out of the stirrups in preparation. My instructor could stand it no longer. She strode across the arena, grabbed Sadie's bridle and pulled her towards the pole. My feet went back into the stirrups and Sadie pranced some more.

'She's not going over. I think, maybe, I'd better get off,' I said to my instructor as I slipped my feet out of the stirrups again.

'DON'T YOU DARE GET OFF THAT HORSE!' my instructor shouted at me. 'You're supposed to be the boss and she's not listening to you. Now give her a whack with your crop, because if you don't, *I* will.'

At that point I didn't know who I was more frightened of – my teacher or my horse. As Sadie finally shot over that garlanded pole, a massive cheer went up from the crowd which had gathered round the gate. With renewed confidence I turned towards the triple which was set out diagonally across the centre of the school. Here, Sadie saved her trump card to last. Faced with the prospect of three poles in quick succession, she decided the only way left to go was… up… and up she reared. I heard someone call out in the background, 'Hi, ho, Silver!'

'What's she doing now!' I cried out, as I leaned forward and grabbed her mane, clinging on for dear life.

'Just get after her and push her forward,' came the order.

Having survived this far gave me the incentive to press on and press on we did, although how we got round that small course I'll never know (I think we missed a few at the end, but hey, who's counting). After what seemed like an endless round, I finally left the arena with my face burning, my confidence drained and the words of my instructor, 'Don't you dare get off that horse!' still ringing in my ears. On the plus side, all the spectators said that mine had been the most entertaining round of the day, and one person said they hadn't had as much fun at a kiddies competition for many a year. Frankly, though, they were five minutes of fame that I could have done without.

I took Sadie's tack off, brushed her down and rugged her up for the night. Now, she was so sweet, nuzzling me as I moved around her, acting like butter wouldn't melt in her mouth; her deep, dark eyes following my every move as I checked her water buckets and popped some carrots and apples in her feed bin. The yard was quiet now and this was our special time together, no pressure to do anything other than be just what we were, a horse and a human. I couldn't resist giving her a big cuddle. I slid one of my arms across her back and the other under her belly, laid my face against the warm softness of her side and hugged her to me, in the closest thing to an embrace that I could manage.

I acknowledged to myself that today's shambles was largely due to rider error and I knew I would go home feeling frustrated at my lack of riding skills. We were working on it, but I still wondered if the day would ever come when I would be any good at riding.

But despite our lack of success in the jump-off, I had to admit to a sneaking admiration for Sadie's proud and fiery character, fighting back against all odds. What a girl! Her defiant nature reminded me a little bit of myself and I loved her all the more for her indomitable spirit. She filled a great chasm in my soul that I had always known was there but had never been able to identify. She was mine and we would work it out, we had the rest of our lives together.

Perhaps it is a good thing that we don't know the mathematics of God's grand design for us, that I didn't know a fuse had been lit and a time bomb was ticking.

CHAPTER 14

Today I found out that Sadie needed a dentist. No sooner had I taken off her stable rug to groom her, than she whipped her head round to the side for a good old scratch. Boy, that must have been some itch, because Sadie gave it such a gnashing with her teeth that when I looked round to see what she was gnawing at, she ripped a piece of top skin off her side. I could barely believe my eyes – exactly where the girth would lie was now a pink patch of oozing flesh.

Now, I had never heard of equine dentists and had no idea when, if ever, Sadie had seen one, but the general consensus was that there must be some very sharp edges on Sadie's teeth to cause such a bad graze. These would need to be filed down and I would have to sort out a dentist's visit in the near future; but first of all, I rinsed off the graze and slapped on a pile of antiseptic cream while it was still fresh and clean.

Unfortunately, the wound was exactly where the line of the girth went, which meant that I wouldn't be able to use a saddle until the graze had healed and I needed to come up with some fresh ideas for Sadie's exercise.

The yard was situated a short distance up a narrow country lane from a small crossroads, and from the gate the views across the undulating countryside were superb. I can't remember whose idea it was, but I thought the suggestion of taking Sadie for a short walk on a lead rope was quite a good one. I thought it would get her used to going out of the school on her own, and we could go down the lane to the crossroads and along the valley road for a few hundred yards. It was a lovely, brisk, sunny day, we wouldn't be gone for long – twenty minutes tops – and we would remain in sight of the school if I needed assistance. Excellent idea!

'You'd better put a bridle on her instead of that headcollar, it will give you more control over the horse…'

'Really?'

'Make her walk on with purpose, and don't let go of the reins,' yet more advice.

'…No, no, I'm sure we'll be fine,' I said confidently.

'Just make sure you *don't* let go of the reins,' was reiterated as I opened the gate.

I gave a little wave, 'Won't be long.'

Sadie seemed hesitant as she came through the gate and was reluctant to follow, but I gripped the reins, one hand close to the bit and the rest of the reins in my other hand, just as I'd been shown earlier. I didn't press her to walk purposefully because we were going downhill and I thought she would be better walking in her own time. On one side of the lane was a hedge, from which Sadie took the occasional nibble, when she spotted something of culinary interest. On the other side was a large field, freshly ploughed with deep, thick, moist furrows of rich brown earth. I breathed in the crisp wintery air and looked out across those yawning furrows, ploughed with such precision, and marvelled at their straightness, while Sadie hopped and skittered along beside me in a most unsettling way, when she wasn't preoccupied with the vegetation. It only took us a few minutes to reach the crossroads at the bottom of the downhill stretch, and we took a right-hand turn, walking parallel to the ploughed field, so that we were still within sight of the riding school. But with no hedge to nibble at and no boundaries other than a shallow ditch on one side, Sadie became even more agitated as I led her further away from her comfort zone.

Horses' eyes are located on the side of their head for a reason; this enables them to see in a wide arc, from front to back, which is important for their survival when spotting predators that try to attack them from the rear. However, humans do not have this type of peripheral vision, so I failed to see what Sadie saw.

Before I knew what was happening, Sadie flung her head high into the air and spun round in a circle. My heart was pounding as I fought to remain in control of the situation, but Sadie threw herself sideways, off the grass verge and down into the ditch that separated the farmer's field from the tarmac country lane.

'DON'T LET GO OF THE REINS!' echoed through my brain and I tightened my grip on them, chanting 'mustn't let go, mustn't let go' to myself. And it was only then that I saw them as well – two riding school horses being led out of the gates by a member of staff. Faced with the option of continuing along the lane with me or the attraction of joining two other horses, Sadie's natural herd instinct proved too much for her. Suddenly she was off… making straight for the yard and the safety of the other horses the quickest way she knew how – straight across the middle of that field.

Those deep, muddy furrows proved to be no obstacle to her, oh no! But me… I managed to keep pace with her for about two strides, before the weight of the thick, sticky mud that clung to my boots anchored my feet to the ground like flies to a flypaper. It all happened in seconds. As Sadie raced off, the reins shot through my hands taking the skin of my palms and fingers with them, and when my hands hit the buckle at the end of the reins, I was launched into the air. I landed legs akimbo, face down in the mud, the reins flew out of my hands and Sadie flew off across the field. Halfway across the field she caught her leg in the flapping reins, pulled up with a start and snorted, head raised to the wind with nostrils flaring. As I looked up, I caught my breath; the split-second image of this beautiful white mare, tail held high, shin deep in the dark earth, silhouetted against a clear, blue winter's sky was burnt onto my brain, like a flash on film, and even to this day, still remains one of my most abiding memories of her.

But the possibility that she might damage her leg or go onto the road as a car came hurtling along caused an adrenalin rush that shot me into orbit and obliterated any pain I might have felt in my hands – that came later. I jumped up, pulled my feet from the viscous mud and made my way across the field, high-stepping the steep furrows with boots squelching at every step from the suction of the mud as it released me. I saw the girl from the yard hurrying towards us to lend a hand, and I approached Sadie as quickly as I could, without startling her. Speaking softly all the time, I gently picked up her leg to release it from the reins and led her gingerly back to the crossroads. She seemed to settle now that we were going towards the other horses and within a few minutes we were back at the yard.

What a sight we must have been… Sadie looked as if she was wearing black socks, and me, I had thick mud all down one side of me, from shoulder to ankle, more was caked over the front of my knees, thighs and chest, and I had even managed to get mud on my face and in my hair.

'Ooh, have you seen Gillian?'

'What happened to you?'

'You're covered in mud!'

'You let go of the reins!'

So would you, I thought to myself, if you were being dragged through the mud at forty miles an hour! And I burst into tears at the sheer relief of having arrived safely back on the yard.

Sadie seemed none the worse for this experience; a quick hosing down soon got rid of all that mud, restoring her legs to their previously pristine white. Before I saw her back into her stable, I checked her over to make sure that there were no cuts or other signs of damage to her legs where she had caught them in the reins. Having satisfied myself that she was still in fine fettle, I left her munching on lunch while I went home for tea and sympathy.

When I walked through the front door, Mike took one look at me, sighed and shook his head from side to side. Before he could say anything, I beat him to it.

'Don't ask!' I said as I chucked my muddy clothes into the dirty linen basket and headed straight for the shower.

Through the rush of water, I heard Mike call out, 'Shall I put the kettle on?' and by the time I was finished, he had a freshly made cup of tea ready and waiting. I sat down, feeling bruised and battered, and updated him on the day's events while he found some plasters for my poor swollen fingers.

Everyone else at the yard thought this event highly amusing, and my sorry tale was told to all and sundry over the following week. Mike just muttered a lot and took over the cooking and washing up for the next few days. After the initial shock I, too, saw the funny side of things and brandished my damaged fingers around like emblems of initiation into the capricious world of the horse owner.

CHAPTER 15

'Try riding her bareback if you can't put a saddle on her.'

Who said that? Yet another bright idea from someone at the yard… But my curiosity was piqued and I'd never ridden bareback before. Where's the harm? I thought. After all, that's why I'd bought her, to have some fun together.

I grabbed my riding hat, popped Sadie's bridle on, had a quick leg-up from a friend before I lost my nerve and we were off.

Riding bareback is such a strange experience. What with Sadie's bony back and my bony bottom, it wasn't particularly comfortable, but I slowly relaxed my body to move in time with her gait. I wobbled a lot at first and held on to Sadie's mane until I found my balance. Without a saddle, I became more aware of the rise and fall of Sadie's shoulder, the natural rhythm of her paces and the seamless movement of her body. I felt every sinew, every muscle, every breath she took as I wrapped my legs tightly around her belly to keep my seat in place; until it seemed we almost melded into one and I felt a closeness to her that I hadn't experienced before.

Sadie took comfort from the presence of another pony having a lesson in the indoor arena at the same time and seemed fairly settled, so I bravely tried a short trot and canter until I began to slide rather precariously to one side. I came back quickly to a walk, discretion being the better part of valour, and we did a few more circuits before finally finishing up. No traumas, no falling off, just lots of fun and I left the yard that day with a real sense of achievement. Lovely!

A few days later the dentist came. I had no idea what to expect so it was with mixed emotions that I greeted him on the yard. Following a brief exchange of pleasantries, he flung open the back of his four-wheel drive and took out a stainless-steel, two-tier trolley together with a rather large leather holdall that appeared to be more like a builder's tool kit than a dentist's bag. I took him round the back to Sadie's stable with that trolley rattling and clanging as it bumped along beside us over the uneven stones of the pathway. Dentist wasted no time in pulling out a metal contraption that looked as if it would be more at home hanging on the wall of a medieval torture chamber than in a dentist's bag, and I stood in awe as he proceeded to fit the device into Sadie's mouth and strap it round her head. This 'gag' appeared to have a ratchet type of mechanism that the dentist cranked up, to open the horse's mouth at the required width for him to set about his work. I was even more amazed to find that Sadie seemed totally unfazed by this new development and stood patiently throughout the examination as Dentist's arm disappeared up to his elbow inside her mouth.

Apparently Sadie hadn't seen a dentist for some time; her jaws didn't line up properly, which meant her teeth were uneven when she ate and there was quite a lot of work to do.

Dentist delivered his verdict: 'Gonna need the drill to sort this lot out.'

'Ooh!' I winced.

He showed me how a horse's teeth go right up the side of their face, and to prove his point he added, 'Go on, put yer hand in 'ere...'

I tentatively put my fingers inside the dark recess of Sadie's gaping mouth for a quick grope.

'Not like that!' he said. 'Put it right up inside, feel up 'er jaw there. Can you feel those sharp bits? That's cos they ain't been ground down by the bottom set when she eats.'

And there was me thinking that a horse only had those few teeth in the front of the mouth.

Normally horses don't need any sedation if they are just having their teeth filed, but if any remedial work needs to be carried out, then a tranquilliser is given. I stood by Sadie's side while the sedative took effect and the dentist got down to business.

'Don't want 'er coming round before I've finished drilling now, do we?' he said, as he pulled out another metallic medieval lookalike from his bag of kit.

He worked quickly, checking the alignment every now and again before he declared, 'That should do the trick!' and was soon steering his trolley away to the other riding school horses that were on his list for a check-up. I kept a watching brief on Sadie as she slowly came round from her anaesthetic while I flitted between stables, watching the dentist at work on his 'regulars'. I was fascinated by the art of equine dentistry and really surprised at how compliant all of the horses seemed to be while the dentist went about his business of strapping this metal frame around their mouths and filing the teeth of those that needed it.

It wasn't long before Sadie's eyes started to open and I could tell she was beginning to come to her senses as she shuffled around her stable unsteadily; she hadn't quite regained control of her tongue, which flopped out from the side of her mouth rather endearingly as she smacked her lips together. I had removed Sadie's hay net and water bucket from her stable before the tranquilliser had been given, so that she wouldn't be tempted to try out her new dental work before she was fully recovered. It would probably be a few hours yet before they could be replaced, when she was no longer in any danger of choking herself.

Before he left, the dentist handed me a newly completed dental record which was to be kept with Sadie's passport and I was advised to make an appointment in about twelve months' time for an annual check-up.

'Any problems in the meantime, just gimme a ring on that number,' he said, handing me his card. And with that, he stashed the trolley in the back of his car, threw the leather bag in with a clunk and was off.

Eventually Sadie was back to her old self again and champing at the bit for her dinner. I served it up, albeit a little later than usual, with an extra helping of carrots so that she could test-drive her new top set. However, the knock-on effect of waiting for Sadie to recover meant that I was also late for dinner. When I got home, it was nothing short of a miracle that I managed to get our evening meal prepared just in time for Mike's arrival. Thank goodness we don't have the dentist every day.

CHAPTER 16

This year, it decided to snow in March. All winter we hadn't had any snow, but now that it was March and we were supposed to be heading into spring, good old England had pulled a fast one and thrown in a late cold spell, just to catch us all out. Under grey skies, the weather was freezing when I arrived at the yard and copious amounts of salt had been strewn around to combat the ice, for the benefit of horses and humans alike. I checked the outdoor arena, and even the small pools of water that gathered in the dips and crevices of the shredded rubber surface had turned to ice.

Today was not a day for hanging about, so after a perfunctory brush down, I tacked Sadie up and headed straight to the indoor school for a quick turn around the arena so that we would be finished before the lunchtime hay was served up. I had an ulterior motive for wanting to be finished before lunch as things tend to get very noisy on the yard at meal times. Usually, the first horse to spot the hay-laden wheelbarrow coming along the yard heralds its pending arrival by making loud, throaty whinnying noises. If that fails to alert the rest of the gang, they turn up the volume by giving the stable door a hefty kicking, which sets everyone else off. With Sadie's hearing tuned finer than a radio mast, I didn't want any early anticipation of the onset of lunch to disrupt our ride, because heaven knows, there were enough likely candidates for causing disruptions as it was.

Anyway, the indoor arena is not totally enclosed but has quite a wide gap along three sides between the top of the wall and the roof, which not only gives a distractingly good view across the adjoining fields but also allows the weather to creep in around the perimeter. This made things interesting for Sadie because she could eyeball the sheep in the field opposite and take

;ue from them if something startled them, or the farmer's sheepdog
ac..ded to herd them off somewhere, causing a raucous baaing to float in
on the breeze. Then there's the odd leaf that blows in, or bird that swoops
through the gap onto one of the beams supporting the roof, any of which
are an excellent excuse for bad behaviour.

Today, however, I noticed the first white flakes as it began to snow and
saw a big snowflake heading for the gap just as we were about to ride by.
A small gust of wind picked it up and blew it straight onto Sadie's nose,
where it promptly melted. Sadie saw it at the last moment and skidded to
a halt as it landed on her, then shook her head in bewilderment as it disappeared into thin air. I could tell from her face that she just couldn't make
it out. I gave her a pat, moved her forward again and wondered if she had
ever seen snow before. I expect she had, but it was probably some while
ago. And when we left the arena shortly afterwards, there was quite a flurry
of snowflakes falling, all cold and wet on Sadie's nose, just like the first one.

Having bought Sadie so late in the year, I had decided to keep her
stabled over that first winter together, for lots of reasons. I didn't know her
history and wasn't sure if she had ever spent a winter outdoors or whether
she would find our winter nights too demanding without the comfort of
a stable. In addition, I thought that she would find it easier to settle into
her new surroundings if she spent a couple of months in her stable, getting
used to the yard routine, notwithstanding the fact that I was also a new
girl who needed to get into a routine. Then there were the practicalities of
allocating my time to look after Sadie and arranging for the livery team to
take over on the days when I couldn't go to the yard. But mostly, from a
personal perspective, I felt more secure having Sadie stabled, knowing that
the riding school staff were always on hand to spot any potential problems
that I hadn't seen coming. The downside of having Sadie stabled was that
she still needed her exercise every day and liked to kick up her heels when
she did come out.

One sunny winter's day, when it was just Sadie and I riding, I decided
to take advantage of the fact that, for once, it wasn't raining and thought
we would go outside for a change. To get to the outdoor arena I had to
pass through two wide metal gates; one leading out of the yard onto the

pathway and the other one at the entrance to the arena. Negotiating the opening and closing of gates on horseback was currently rather low down on my agenda, having prioritised improving my basic riding skills for the time being; neither did I want to ask any of the staff, who were busy mucking out stables, to give me a hand, so I led Sadie through the gates. Having firmly closed the arena gate behind us, we walked across to a bank on the far side, which I was going to use to mount up from. I brought Sadie to a halt alongside it and checked her girth to make sure the saddle was secure; I pulled down the stirrup on one side, walked round to adjust the stirrup on the other side and, without warning, Sadie's head shot into the air, ears pricked forward. I should have guessed that something was up, but before I could react, she was away... cantering full pelt across the arena, empty stirrups flapping against the sides of the saddle. I just stood there, hands on hips, in the vortex of her slipstream and watched. A few seconds later, one of the girls from the yard came running down the path towards the arena.

'Gillian, are you all right?' she gasped.

'Yes, I'm fine, thanks,' I called back.

'Only we saw Sadie flying around the arena with no rider on her, and we thought you'd fallen off.'

'Fallen off?' I said. 'I haven't had a chance to get on her yet! But thanks for coming down,' I replied.

'Oh, as long as you're all right.'

Perhaps it was a good job I didn't have time to mount up, I thought to myself, and decided that maybe it was a better idea if I went and collected a lunge rope to allow her to let off steam before we tried to do any more riding that day...

But it was comforting to know that if I was lying prostrate on the ground, someone from the school was looking out for me.

CHAPTER 17

Despite the unseasonal cold snap we had just had, Sadie's winter coat was coming out by the handful. At first, I was confused by this loss of hair, until someone explained to me that the change of coat from winter to summer is triggered by the increase in daylight hours and not by the daily temperatures. So it made no difference to Sadie that we'd had some recent snow; the days were growing longer and she was shedding her coat. Whenever I started to brush her, great clouds of white hair would billow up from her back, like a snow storm, and even if I stood downwind from her, I still got smothered in hair. No matter how hard I tried to tidy myself up before I went home, those white hairs stuck to my clothes like glue and almost seemed to permeate the fibres. In an effort to contain the spread of hairs, I took my outer clothing off before I went in through the front door, gave it a good shake and separated my horse clothes from the rest of the washing. But even that old trick of using Sellotape to pick up the loose hairs off clothing was hard-pressed to make a difference to the spread of white hair through our bungalow. Unfortunately, the situation was compounded by our cat, Meli, who is also mostly white, apart from her black tail and a few random splodges across her back. Her thick fur is invitingly soft with a fine layer of downy underhair that flies from her coat at the slightest touch.

Mike's household had been sadly lacking in the pet department before he met me, something I was determined to rectify as soon as we started living together. For me, living with animals was as essential as having a meal each day. As an urban resident, they were the antidote to my alienation from the natural world and fundamental to the restoration of my sanity when I closed my front door on the madness of modern-day living.

Mike's initial objections to household pets amounted to the mention of animal hairs and a gentle reminder about the destructive properties of cat pee on the garden plants I had so tenderly nurtured.

'We won't get a Persian cat, if you're worried about hairs all over the place, and we can put a litter tray in the utility room for her to use instead of the garden. Cats don't like getting their feet dirty and some of them prefer a nice clean box to pee in, especially if it's raining outside,' I said, sweeping away Mike's half-hearted protestations like a bulldozer on a building site, burying them as I went.

A few days later we picked up our first feline from a rescue centre; the flotsam of a broken marriage, cast aside like the husband, while the kids and other pets were moved to pastures new by the wife.

She was a funny little thing; antisocial, introverted and fearful, and I responded immediately to her vulnerability by falling in love with her. I decided to name her Melina, after the late, great Greek actress; a strong, passionate woman who gave joy to so many people with her film and stage performances and who later, as Minister for Culture, campaigned so ardently for the return of the Elgin Marbles to their homeland. I had hoped that some of the vibrancy of her namesake would rub off on my shy, nervous adoptee, but she went on to spend the first fortnight in her new home under the dining room table – only breaking cover for secret night-time forays into the kitchen for a hasty meal and a toilet break.

Time brought Meli the understanding that life wasn't so bad after all, and with the move to our new bungalow, she blossomed. As did her coat. It grew thicker and longer and more luxurious than any I had seen before, and renewed itself with such vigour that I thought she'd end up bald. When she scratched behind her ear, fur flew out in great wads, like stuffing from a pillow.

'There's half a cat on the living room carpet,' Mike would say when he got up in the morning. 'I thought you said that short-haired cats don't shed any hair…'

I regarded these comments with disdain, giving them the contempt they deserved by refusing to respond, but I did take the precaution of covering the settee with a bath towel when we were out so that there was a hair-free seat to sit on in the evening.

As the springtime moult began in earnest, Mike found an excess of white hair on every available surface.

'There are even hairs in the washing machine,' he complained, plucking a white hair from his briefs as he hung them on the dryer.

Whilst the cat was culpable to a certain extent, I had to admit to Mike that, with the addition of a white horse to the fold, there was now another culprit who was at least as guilty as our poor Meli.

'It won't be for long, Mike, as soon as she gets her summer coat through, she'll stop moulting,' I said, trying to smooth the situation over after Mike had sat on our settee in his suit trousers and got up with a bum covered in hair.

'Who are we talking about now?' Mike replied. 'The cat or the horse?'

'Well, both of them, I suppose,' I said.

'It's bad enough with the cat's hair, now we've got white horse hair everywhere as well…'

'Yeh, I know, honey,' I commiserated. 'But that's what happens when you have animals…'

In order to alleviate the situation, I decided to tackle the cleaning on a more frequent basis and it wasn't until our Hoover started to whine and groan from the unfamiliar onslaught, that I realised it hadn't been emptied for ages. When I did look inside, it was so full up with horse hair I could've stuffed an armchair with it – although I wasn't about to start a cottage industry at this stage of my life.

The tantalising warmth of a sunny spring day turned my thoughts to summer and I looked forward to sharing those months with Sadie. Our first summer together, when we could wander the lanes and forest bridleways with the warmth of the sun on our backs, flowers in the hedgerows and the smell of freshly cut grass in the air. Those are the sort of days that make you feel good just to be alive, make you appreciate everything you have and why I'd bought a horse to share them with.

CHAPTER 18

Today, Sadie and I parted company. I was in the riding school's office, casting my eye over the daily diary for the indoor arena, when I spotted a small group scheduled for later that morning. No problem there, I thought: only a few kids booked and with their combined ages barely adding up to my own, that particular lesson was bound to be well within my comfort zone as far as technical ability was concerned. Added to that was my renewed confidence in Sadie, following our practice sessions on the lunge, and I made the snap decision to join the class. Yes, I thought, this should be right up our alley. Well, you know what they say about assumption being the mother of all…

The first half of the lesson went smoothly, and in the second half, our instructor decided to spice things up a little by placing a pole on the ground for the kids to go over. Yes, I know I said I wasn't interested in learning to jump or anything like that, but I had been seduced by the excitement that even the smallest of hurdles now generated and was eager to show how well Sadie and I were progressing. The horses all seemed 'up' for it and we set off one behind the other, picking up quite a turn of speed down the straight. The first two horses hopped over the pole with barely a break in their stride, and then it was our turn. I honestly don't know what Sadie thought she was doing, it was only a pole on the ground, but she launched herself over it like it was three feet high. She stretched her neck forward and down, pulling the reins almost out of my hands, shot her bottom in the air and catapulted me straight off, over her head. I landed with a thud, most ungraciously, with my legs in the air and my face in the dirt, whilst the rest of the class looked on in horror.

'Are you all right?' called the instructor as I sat there for a second or two, trying to catch my breath.

'Yes, I'm fine,' I squeaked, feeling bruised and tender in more places than I cared to mention.

The only adult in a class full of kids and I'm the one on the ground. I felt my face burn with indignity – oh, the shame of it! Worst of all, I knew that I would now have to follow protocol. Etiquette dictates that if a rider falls off their steed, they must get straight back on – barring serious injury, of course. With five pairs of eyes boring into me and the instructor breathing down my neck, there was no escape. I had about as much enthusiasm for getting back on Sadie as I had for sitting on a cactus, but reluctantly, I brushed myself off and remounted. Next time around we took a slow walk over the pole and fortunately the lesson finished shortly after that, sparing me any further embarrassment.

Back on the yard I gingerly dismounted.

'You don't bounce so easily as you get older,' I said to the proprietor as I put my saddle away and thought longingly of the soothing soak in a hot bath that I'd promised myself as soon as I got home.

There's an old wives' tale that says you need to fall off at least three times before you can call yourself a rider. I've had my three spills and more since then and I remain unconvinced that I'm a better rider for it – surely the whole point of learning to ride is staying on?

All through the difficulties, I never once regretted buying Sadie. None of us knew why she was as she was, although we had many discussions on possible reasons for Sadie's fear and mistrust when being ridden. By contrast, she was a lovely mare to look after, good in her stable, never nipped or kicked out, loved being groomed, didn't mind having her coat clipped in the winter or being rinsed off with the hosepipe, but she had become jaded when ridden. Heaven knows what had happened to her in previous lives, but she had learnt that misbehaving was the best way to avoid doing anything that she didn't want to do, or was frightened to do.

'You don't have to keep her, you know,' one of the girls on the yard said. 'You could try selling her on to someone else.'

I knew that Sadie's original buyer, looking for a nice 'quiet' mare, would never have kept her; that she would have been sold on yet again, probably resulting in an escalation of bad behaviour. I thought of all those 'accidental' twists and turns in our lives that had brought us together, just at the point where Sadie needed someone and I was open to a change in my life. I felt that this chance event was more than a coincidence and that, for reasons neither of us understood, it was Sadie's destiny to be with me. My response was immediate.

'No, I'll never sell her. She's mine and I love her. No matter what she does, I'll never part with her, not in a million years.'

As well as her aversion to ridden work, Sadie was quite domineering on the lead rope. If something took her fancy while I was leading her across the yard she would veer off at a tangent, ignoring me completely. Whenever she came in from the field her first priority was to check out her stable for food. She would walk quietly along beside me, feigning disinterest until we reached the fork in the pathway that led to her stable, then she would barge down that turning, dragging me along behind her without a 'by your leave'. I would dig my heels in and brace myself against the rope, but she would power on regardless, pulling me off balance. It wasn't until I had my own horse that I realised how powerful these animals are; even the smallest pony can pull you off your feet, if they've a mind to.

It was time for a little respect, so I decided to try some ground control exercises, in addition to our ridden work, to induce a more compliant attitude from Sadie.

Long into the evening I researched equine training techniques on the internet, finding not only plenty of reading material but video footage as well. I also spent an afternoon browsing local bookshops for something suitable and came up with a wealth of information on all aspects of behaviour and training. I finally made my choice and armed with a 'basics book' highlighted and annotated at the relevant exercises, I returned to the yard full of optimism.

But Sadie wasn't a young horse and she had spent a long time learning bad habits. Books are all very well as background, but it is experience that fills in the blanks and I had very little of that. Every time I visited Sadie we spent ten minutes on the lead rope before our ride. With a lot of patience, Sadie gradually consented to walk around poles or execute a 'figure of eight', but we skipped the exercises on reversing – she didn't need any practice in that direction.

Despite our progress in these sessions, Sadie's performance was only marginally improved on the yard, especially when a more appealing proposition presented itself. Soon my idealistic expectations became tempered by a more practical, realistic approach, and the more I got to know Sadie, the easier it became to pre-empt the bad behaviour before it happened. I would keep my eyes peeled for decoys such as feed buckets languishing in forgotten corners, knowing that Sadie would make a beeline for them if she could, and I positioned myself to block her view of whatever item of irresistibility beckoned. It didn't always work, but with perseverance I was able to achieve a modicum of success. I was always open to suggestion, but I think the best piece of advice I received was to make sure that whatever we were doing, we always finished on a good note. 'Quit while you're ahead' became my motto from that day on and I have found this advice invaluable, not only with Sadie, but with other aspects of my life as well.

Following Sadie's purchase, there was still money left in my Mercedes fund, which I referred to, jokingly, as 'Sadie's savings'. One afternoon, while I was sitting at the kitchen table with Mike, I asked him to make me a promise.

'If anything ever happens to me…' I began.

'Nothing's going to happen to you, darling,' Mike butted in.

'No, honey, just listen, I'm being serious. If anything ever happens to me, promise me that you will never sell Sadie. She's to be kept at the yard, where they know how to look after her, and you must use the savings fund to pay for her keep.'

Mike looked at me intently for a second or two before nodding his consent.

And I left my horse in the hands of the person that I trusted most in this world, knowing that come hell or high water, he would keep his promise.

CHAPTER 19

Today I found out that besides the birds and the leaves and the wind and poles and boxes and rubbish bins and plastic bags and noisy machinery (is there anything I've forgotten…?) there is also something else that Sadie is frightened of.

At the bottom of the lane there is a household that keeps two donkeys. Sometimes they are nowhere to be seen (probably in their stables) and at other times they are out in a field that runs parallel to the lane. Now these must be two of the most inoffensive creatures I think I have ever seen; no running backwards and forwards from these chaps, no bucking or bad habits, nor any other form of riotous behaviour to my knowledge, just plain, minding-my-own-business grass grazers.

Down the lane I go with Sadie in complete ignorance of this hitherto unrealised phobia when, suddenly, she skids to a halt. Though not an unusual occurrence in itself, I could see that she had her peepers firmly fixated on these two strange horse-yet-not-horse-like creatures. They looked at her and she looked at them until she couldn't stand the suspense of the unknown any longer and tried to make a bolt for home. Up we went onto the roadside bank, dodging the telegraph pole as we weaved in and out, and I tried desperately to regain control of her to turn her back onto our original course. But she was having none of it. Every time I turned her towards the donkeys, she veered off every which way she could – she trembled and shook and I held my breath, hoping that the donkeys would at least have the decency to remain silent within earshot of Sadie. One bray from them and I knew it would all end in disaster. In a last-ditch attempt to get her to walk past the donkeys, I dismounted and tried leading her. This, unfortunately, was my biggest mistake of all, because at ground level you have virtually no control over a petrified horse and she was up the bank again quicker than greased lightening. Sadie had obviously never met a donkey before, and I could tell that she was genuinely frightened of them as I patted my lathered horse and tried to calm her down. I reassessed the situation and decided that sometimes the forces of nature are truly stacked against us. I took pity on Sadie's heaving sides and sweaty flanks, and I decided to give in gracefully rather than make the situation worse; I would ask for advice and maybe a slow introduction might make a difference. I remounted, gave her one last look at the donkeys, walked a few circles and headed for home. Sometimes, I think, you need to know when to take a step back – after all, in my book there's no dishonour in a dignified retreat.

Back at the yard, I elicited advice from anyone willing to listen and we all put our thinking caps on. Following this latest escapade, the 'donkey dilemma' (as it was known) became topic of the week.

The first and most obvious solution was a 'donkey detour', but whilst this was okay as a temporary measure, it was hardly the solution I had in mind. Various ideas were bandied about over the next couple of days, but in the end, the favourite of them all was to recruit the services of that most dependable mare – Nobelle. A 'donkey stratagem' was devised that required precision timing to succeed and, as we hatched our dastardly plan, I decided that the next time Donna and I went out, we would put it to the test.

A few days later I had my window of opportunity.

'Fancy a quick hack round the block, Donna?' I said.

'Why not?' she replied, as I explained my donkey dilemma.

Donna and I tacked up with trepidation, would it be success… or failure? We would soon find out. One of the girls opened the gate for us, wished me 'good luck' and watched as we walked briskly down the lane.

On the approach to the donkey field we took up our positions – Nobelle walked along the side of the lane that was the closest to the field and I brought Sadie up, alongside Nobelle on the inside, so that Nobelle and Donna were blocking Sadie's view of the offending creatures. Then, just as we came alongside the actual corner of the field, we moved swiftly up a gear, shot straight into trot and sped past the donkeys before Sadie could bat an eye! Now that's what I mean about being cunning.

Every horse is different; they all have their own individual likes and dislikes and Sadie was no exception: she had a great character and could be quite mischievous. As soon as the warmer spring weather started to nudge its way onto the calendar, the owners of the yard liked to spruce up the place with tubs of flowers and strategically placed hanging baskets full of colourful plants. I mention the word 'strategic' because most horses like eating flowers and will polish them off in two seconds flat if they get the chance. So the hanging baskets were usually placed high enough to be out of reach of the average-sized riding school horse, where they would sway on the breeze, tantalisingly wafting their scent only inches from a horse's grasp.

We were now well into April and I noticed that someone had been hard at work planting up the old baskets with an array of recently purchased plants that were just coming into flower. I had been in a group lesson that morning which had gone fairly well, and as I dismounted, I noticed that one of the freshly planted baskets had been placed on a chair by the tack room door, in preparation for hanging. It caught my eye because of the splash of colour coming from one of the new plants, a lovely polyanthus, where the flower-wielding stalk had produced three perfect blooms in a striking, vibrant yellow. My instructor followed the ride out of the school and, as she passed by, we had a quick chat about Sadie's progress. She was still talking to me as she grabbed a saddle from one of the horses that had finished the ride and walked towards the tack room with it. I followed her for a couple of steps to catch the last snatches of the conversation, while Sadie shuffled along behind me. As my instructor disappeared into the darkness of the tack room doorway to put the saddle away, I stood for a few seconds pondering her words. Just then, I felt the almost imperceptible brush of Sadie's head against my back and something in that movement made me turn round sharply – just in time to see Sadie's quivering lips clamp down on those beautiful, luscious blooms. I caught my breath in horror as she gave one forceful tug and ripped the whole plant right out of the basket, stalk dangling from her mouth while the ragged roots rained particles of potting soil onto the concrete yard below. As quickly as I could, I ripped the remains of that poor deflowered plant from Sadie's slobbering mouth and stuffed it back into the hole left behind, in the still moist soil of the hanging basket, from whence it had come. I had just finished gently pressing the soil in around the leaves of the polyanthus when my eagle-eyed instructor came out of the tack room.

She looked first at the basket, then at me and finally at Sadie. She clocked Sadie's mouth still frothy with green-tinged saliva and said, rather pointedly, 'There were *three* flowers on that plant!'

'Were there?' I replied, in an effort to remain non-committal and, avoiding her gaze, I turned quickly to Sadie and said, 'Come on, girl, time to get you back to your stable.' We beat a hasty retreat round the back of the yard, where I couldn't suppress a guilty giggle any longer.

CHAPTER 20

With the warmer weather settling in, I decided that it was time for Sadie to be 'turned out' along with most of the other horses. From a personal perspective, I wanted my horse to live as near as natural an existence as possible, spending most of her time in a field as part of a herd. This doesn't suit every horse, particularly the finer breeds, and some horses are unable to live 'out' if they have allergies or are prone to certain medical conditions where their grazing has to be restricted. But I wouldn't know if Sadie would be happy living out until I tried it.

A short walk down the lane, there was a twelve-acre field where around seven or eight mares belonging to the riding school were turned out together. Now I wasn't sure what an acre was (should have paid more attention at school), but twelve of them make a very large field indeed, and this one was perfect for Sadie. It had trees and a tall hedgerow on one side, providing shelter from the wind and shade from the sun, as well as the shell of an old brick building, which would also offer protection when the weather was bad. Large metal troughs at one end provided fresh drinking water and there was plenty to eat with the spring grass now coming through thick and fast.

I discussed my plan to turn Sadie out, with the yard owner. Horses have a herd hierarchy, and when a horse is introduced into an established herd, the newcomer is often kept on the periphery of the group until the rest of the horses accept it. If any of the herd take a dislike to the newcomer, they can assert their superiority by kicking and other aggressive behaviour, so I was warned that Sadie may have to take a few 'knocks' from the others before she settled in. We decided to turn Sadie and Nobelle out first, and then introduce the other mares gradually throughout the day. Hopefully they wouldn't gang up on her.

On Sunday morning we walked Nobelle and Sadie the short distance to the field and, as soon as the gate closed behind us, we set them loose. Quick as a flash, Nobelle spun round on those big, black, sturdy legs of hers and cantered off, bucking with a joie de vivre only the feeling of freedom can give. Sadie hesitated for only a second before she sped off in hot pursuit. They didn't go far, and just as abruptly as they had cantered off, they came to a halt, stuck their noses in the grass and started to eat, oblivious to all and sundry. As the rest of the horses went up to the field, I spent some time by the gate, just in case there was any aggressive behaviour, but fortunately our plan worked perfectly.

Occasionally during those first few weeks, there was a scuffle in the field and Sadie would come back to the yard with the odd cut or graze. But it soon became evident that she was quite capable of sticking up for herself, and it wasn't long before she became an established member of the 'gang' in her own right.

During those pleasant hours spent in the field, Sadie struck up another unlikely friendship with a robust black cob from the riding school, called Cleo. Again, these two mares were as different from each other as chalk from cheese, but Cleo would prove to be as loyal and protective a friend to Sadie as she could ever have wished for.

All my fears about turning Sadie out vanished in the wind because she took to living out like a duck to water. She loved that field. I know she did, because when she was out, it became the devil's own job to bring her in again.

Initially she tried to communicate her disapproval of being brought in by instigating a stop-start charade. Once I had the headcollar on she would walk behind me for a few yards, then stop, then walk a few more steps, then stop again – you get my drift? And this would go on all the way back to the gate. Once we were outside the field it was like 'game over' and Sadie would walk perfectly normally along the lane back to the school. If she happened to be close to the gate when I arrived, I was in with the chance of a quick exit, but if the horses were over on the far side of the field, my heart would sink.

After a few weeks of the stop-start schematics, Sadie decided it was time to up the ante. The next time I went to the field, I opened the gate as usual, called her name and walked towards her. Sadie carried on grazing. When I got to within a few yards of her, she slowly moved away, and when she felt that she had put an adequate distance between us, she started grazing again. The first time it happened, I didn't really think about it, just walked on that bit further, but when Sadie moved the second time, I felt a creeping unease. I increased my pace and just managed to sneak up on her before she moved a third time.

Phew! I thought to myself, just got the headcollar on in time, we'll be all right now we're headed back to the gate. But that woman's brain must have been working overtime, because halfway there, Sadie twisted sharply to her right, ripped the lead rope out of my hands and galloped off – only coming to a halt when she stood on the end of her lead rope and nearly tripped herself up. I ran after her, puffing and blowing, and quickly grabbed the rope before she could work out how to release herself. Once more I made my way back towards the gate; but remember, we are talking twelve acres here and I was a long, long way from that exit. In fact, it might just as well have been a million miles away for all the difference that it made because every time the exit loomed, Sadie galloped off.

I became so cross and frustrated, I didn't know what to do. In a battle of strength and stamina, Sadie would win hands down, and at this rate, I'd be running around the field all day! Tempting her with food or titbits wasn't an option because I'd get mobbed by the other horses, and I was stumped for any other ideas.

With her headcollar still on and the rope trailing behind her, Sadie turned her attention back to grazing, completely unfazed by this turn of events. There was nothing else for it. I walked back to the school.

The girls spotted me coming, empty-handed.

'Where have you been?' one of them said.

'I thought you were bringing Sadie in from the field?' piped up some-one else.

I started to reply and got as far as, 'So did I…' before I burst into tears.

'What's happened now?'

'I'm not really crying,' I said, searching madly in my pocket for a bit of old tissue to wipe my nose with. 'I'm just so frustrated. I couldn't catch the b★#★!?! I haven't even got the headcollar,' I continued. 'She's still wearing it, I couldn't get close enough to take it off!'

'We'll soon see about that,' said a friend. 'I'll come with you to the field. You can't let her get away with that! It's all about discipline, you see.'

Ten minutes later I returned to the field with reinforcements. With the headcollar still on, Sadie was easier to catch, and with someone either side of her, we finally made it across the field and out of the gate. As I have said before, brute strength on its own is never enough; technique and cunning are much better allies.

However, by now it had taken me so long to bring Sadie in from the field, I didn't have enough time left to go for a ride. Instead, I gave her a good brush all over and a small feed, by way of a bribe for coming to the yard, before I took her back to the field again!

None of the other mares were like this. I would look on with chagrin when other owners went up to the field and only had to call their horse before it came cantering up to the gate to greet them.

So, again I sought advice. I swapped her headcollar for a bridle when collecting her from the field because I had more control with a bridle. Another ruse was to bring Sadie in with another horse, especially if it was Nobelle, and I had a degree of success with this approach. I tried to make Sadie's experience at the yard a positive one, by feeding her and giving her small treats, such as carrots and apples, in the hope that she would associate these titbits with the yard and therefore be easier to catch. But for Sadie, there was no incentive sweet enough to make coming in from the field any less of an ordeal for her, and me, for that matter.

However, I found out purely by chance that there was one sure-fire way guaranteed to bring Sadie in from the field without a murmur – and that was to pretend to leave her on her own.

One morning there were only three horses in the field: Sadie and two others. I went to fetch Sadie, along with one of the girls from the school who was collecting the other two. My friend collected her horses in seconds and the three of them stood patiently by, while I ran round in circles trying to catch Sadie.

After ten minutes or more she called to me, 'Here, Gillian. Come and take one of these horses and walk back to the gate with me. Leave Sadie to get on with it, she won't stay here on her own.'

'Are you sure?' I said, not entirely convinced.

'I'm positive. She will not stay here without the others.'

'Okay, it's worth a try,' I said, and I pushed Sadie's bridle onto my shoulder, turned my back on her and walked across to the others.

Sadie looked on suspiciously while we walked the other two horses casually across to the gate. Sadie stared on intently. We got further and further away from her and still she remained motionless. Then suddenly, just as we arrived at the gate, she came hurtling across the field, hooves drumming on the ground like pistons, to join us.

'I told you she wouldn't want to be left behind, didn't I?' the other girl said with a smile, as I casually slipped the bridle over Sadie's head.

In the end, Sadie's natural herd instinct had triumphed over everything and even the loveliness of her field had paled into insignificance when faced with the prospect of being alone. It was just a pity that I couldn't use that ploy every time I went to collect her.

CHAPTER 21

A few days later I pulled onto the yard and realised the farrier had arrived – now there's another time-honoured trade that I've found fascinating.

I'd forgotten it was shoeing day, but as soon as I stepped out of the car the distinctive smell from a plume of smoke drifting my way announced the farrier's presence. The knowledge and skills of a farrier are often handed down from father to son and the principles of shoeing today vary little from those of yesteryear, apart from the portability of certain items. The huge old furnaces used to transform solid iron into molten metal now appear in the guise of small 'ovens' heated by gas canisters in the back of the farrier's van and the heavy anvils come in more manageable sizes. On average, a farrier working alone can replace the shoes of seven to eight horses per day, and our yard had a regular farrier who came each week.

I was amazed to learn that the average horse needs a new set of shoes roughly every six weeks, so all the horses on our yard are dealt with on a rota basis. Usually it's the rate of growth of the horn on the horses' hooves that dictates the frequency of shoeing. In fact, there was one horse at the yard, whose feet grew quicker than most, who needed a change of shoes every four weeks; another little expense that soon racks up the overall cost of keeping a horse. If the shoes aren't removed and the horn is allowed to grow, a horse will quickly go lame.

Today it was Sadie's turn to see the farrier, so I brought her round from her stable and tied her up on the yard, to take her place in line with the other horses. One look from the farrier told me that Sadie's hooves were in good shape, but she needed a new set of shoes and her feet trimmed. I stayed to watch as he set to work removing the old shoes. He'd barely started when the yard owner's dogs appeared from out of nowhere and started vying for position close by.

'Oh, look!' I said. 'The dogs have turned up; I wonder what they're after.'

The farrier smiled and said, 'You'll soon see,' and he started to trim back the excess horn from the foot.

As the pieces of horn fell to the floor, the stealthy arrival of the dogs became clear – they darted in, snatched up the large slivers and ran off to a quiet corner. There, they clasped the pieces of horn between their paws and chewed on them with the same relish as a prize bone.

'Do they always do that?' I asked, astounded.

'Yep, every time,' said the farrier.

Dogs racing around with bits of horn poking out of their mouths are all part and parcel of shoeing day, as is the singular smell that emanates from the smouldering new shoes as they sizzle on the horse's hoof whilst the farrier tests the fit. There is something about that pungent, unmistakeable aroma that appeals to my senses, much the same as creosote used to when I was a child. I can still remember walking past a freshly creosoted fence on my way to school and lingering in the pall of the heavy odour that still hung in the air from a weekend's work.

But shoeing is hard work and farriers need to keep their wits about them when dealing with horses. From the dull clank of the hammer on heavy metal as the shoes are pounded into shape, to the weight of the horses' feet as they rest on his tough leather-aproned lap while he firmly nails the new shoe into place, a farrier needs to look after his own feet as well as those of the horse – call it an occupational hazard if you will, but a farrier with his foot in plaster tends to lose an awful lot of business…

Ever had a horse stand on your foot? No, neither had I until I had Sadie, and I can assure you, it is excruciating. Think of a ton of horse flesh, all heavy muscle and bone, put an iron shoe on the end, and there you have it!

It happened one day when I was having one of my close encounters with Sadie. I was brushing her neck and smoothing her coat, oblivious to the impending doom, when she shifted her weight slightly and wham, that ton of horse flesh, that I mentioned earlier, came down like a mallet, right on my toes.

'My foot! My foot!' I screamed, and the shrill octave of my voice startled Sadie enough for her to shuffle her hooves again and release my foot. Unfortunately, that didn't stop the pain. It's like someone has thrust your toes into a vice, tightened the screws and forgotten to release you. I jumped up and down on one foot, tears in my eyes, waiting for the pain to subside, but my toes throbbed like a chorus of drums.

Needless to say, I cut my visit short that day.

'What's up?' the yard manager asked, when she saw the pained expression on my face.

I pointed to my foot.

'Ah!' she said knowingly.

'I'm off home,' I said through clenched teeth.

'Don't take your boots off 'till you get there, otherwise you might not get them back on again if your toes swell up,' she warned.

'Great!' I muttered to myself as I hobbled over to my car, which fortunately has an automatic gearbox, otherwise I might not have been able to drive at all.

I eased my boot off when I got home, prodded my toes gingerly and ran cold water over them for a few minutes in an attempt to reduce the swelling. I found an old bandage and wrapped it around my toes, more for support than any realistic expectation of mending them, and decamped to the settee to watch TV for the rest of the day.

It was in this supine position, with my foot resting on top of the coffee table, that Mike found me when he came in from work.

'What has happened now?' he said without preamble.

'Sadie stood on my foot, honey,' I replied.

We took off the bandage and checked out the toes, which were taking on a nice purple hue already, but nothing looked broken. Mike was happily commiserating with me until I told him that I couldn't stand on one leg long enough to cook the dinner so he would have to take over for a day or two, although I was very happy to assist him.

'How do you think you're going to manage that?' he said.

'Well, at least I can peel some potatoes while I'm sitting here,' I said, trying to be helpful.

My toes went through a pretty array of colours, from purple to yellow over the next week, but it could have been a lot worse. As soon as I was back in action, I headed straight for the nearest retailers of working men's boots and ordered a solid pair of steel toe-caps. Those boots have been the mainstay of my riding kit; they've seen me through the foulest of weather and were worth every penny I paid for them. I've had horses inadvertently tread on my feet several times since then (it's so easily done, especially when you're dealing with an excited horse), and those boots have spared me from broken bones many times over.

CHAPTER 22

June brought with it the hottest weather that year. I am a warm-weather person and I love those long, hot, lazy summer days that can be such a treat when our otherwise unpredictable English climate refuses to follow the seasonal guidelines. But warm weather has its drawbacks; one of them being an upsurge of flies that enjoy nothing better than supping on a sweaty horse. So after our ride that day, I decided it was time that Sadie had a proper bath, instead of the usual quick wipe down.

I assembled my gear: horse shampoo, separate conditioner for mane and tail, buckets, sponges (separate one for the face) and sweat scraper (a bit like a rubber windscreen wiper with a handle), to remove the excess water. I positioned Sadie next to the hosepipe and set to work.

'Wash her like you would your own hair,' I had been told. 'Get her wet, put shampoo on and massage it in with a good sponge; then rinse off with clean water, making sure you get *all* the shampoo out of the coat.'

Shampooing was easy, but rinsing off was more tricky, especially when I tried to rinse the shampoo out of Sadie's mane, which is above head height for me. I ended up having as much water sprayed over me as Sadie had over her; annoyingly, some of the water from the hosepipe ran straight down the length of my arm to my armpit, where gravity took over to wet the rest of me. Sadie behaved perfectly throughout and only remonstrated when I tried to wet her face, so I just wiped it over with a damp sponge. By the time I'd finished, I was soaked, but it was worth it and I stepped back to admire my afternoon's work.

'Enjoy!' one of the girls said cheerfully as she walked by, 'she won't stay like that for long, not once she goes back to the field.'

'Maybe not,' I said, but I didn't care. Her hooves glistened, her coat shone and her mane and tail sparkled in the sunlight. To me, she looked like a million dollars.

Afterwards we took a leisurely stroll back to the field, where I turned Sadie loose, secured the gate and stopped to rest my arms on the top bar for a few minutes. I laid my chin on my hands and drank in the scene as Sadie trotted over to rejoin the other horses. Under a clear blue sky the clarity of light intensified the colours of nature and I looked out across a palette of greens. I closed my eyes and breathed in deeply, filling my lungs with country air, laden with the scent of wild flowers. A warm feeling of contentment washed over me as I realised that I had been able to offer this vulnerable horse a good home, where I knew she was happy. Fresh from her bath, Sadie stood out amongst the other brown horses in the field, and as the light kissed her back, I thought that her coat took on an almost luminescent quality – like a pearl. Yes, I thought, she looked just like a pearl, a pearl amongst the daisies, floating in a sea of deep green grass.

CHAPTER 23

D id I mention that horses have two blind spots: one just below and to the front of their nose, and the other one right behind their backside? Well, I found a third.

We commented on the weather that day; it was fine and mostly clear with just a few of those fluffy, white, cotton wool clouds floating across a cerulean sky – perfect weather for Mike's regular ramble. He enjoys walking, you see, and a few of his like-minded colleagues from work had set up a rambling group. Every once in a while the office troop would don their hiking boots and head off across the footpaths and byways of Kent, along a variety of routes normally punctuated by a pub or two. This time, their route was to cut across the south-eastern cliffs, through National Trust land, taking in some spectacular coastal scenery and an obligatory watering hole along the way.

Shortly after breakfast, before we went our separate ways, Mike asked rhetorically, 'You won't be needing me at all, will you? Because I shall be gone most of the day.'

'No, honey,' I responded. 'I'm going to the riding school this morning, and I'll probably pop round to Mum's later on in the afternoon for a cup of tea. You enjoy your walk, and I'll see you later on tonight.'

This summer there seemed to be a surge in the numbers and varieties of flies in the area, causing everyone on the yard to speculate about mild winters, global warming and the life cycle of flying insects. Whether or not there was any connection between them all, the fact remained that horse flies were out in force, driving all the horses nuts as they stood stamping their feet and swishing their tails, while those pesky varmints zoned in on every square inch that hadn't been sprayed or wiped down with any one of the myriad makes of horse fly deterrent currently on the market. Sadie hated them just as much as all the other horses did and stamped her feet irately when she felt those big, grey bloodsuckers nipping at her skin, and today was no exception.

After our ride I wiped Sadie down with a wet flannel, sponging off the patches of sweat, particularly under her legs and around the saddle and girth area. By the time I had put her saddle and bridle away, her coat was dry enough for a quick 'once over' with the brush to smooth it all down. I bent down to finish off her feet, and whilst I was down there I took a quick look under her body just to make sure I hadn't missed anything. That was when I thought I caught a glimpse of a light spot of something on the inside of her back leg, the one that was on the opposite side from me. It could have been a spot of dried mud I'd missed or just a fleck of bedding stuck to her leg but whatever it was, we'll never know, because that was when I found it – the third blind spot, that is – which is centrally located right underneath a horse's belly.

What I should have done was walk round to the other side of Sadie, the side that the leg with the offending particle was on; but oh no… I thought, I can get that spot from here… if I just lean that little bit further under Sadie's big, round stomach, stretch my arm out with the brush and… Crack! Something hit me like a sledge hammer, right across the side of my head, catching my temple and the orbital bone of my eye, and I knew instinctively it was serious.

I used to watch those cartoon programmes as a kid, where one of the characters gets hit on the head and a circle of stars rotates around them as they sway woozily from side to side. Well, that's exactly how I felt. I had bent down under Sadie's tummy just as she had taken a swipe at a fly with her iron-clad back hoof, and the split-second timing of the kick had caught me fair and square on the side of my head. I don't actually remember an awful lot after that, but one of the girls on the yard saw me apparently reel back from Sadie, clutching my head, and stagger along for a few paces before collapsing on the block of bricks used by the riders to mount their horses.

One of them rushed over and said, 'Are you all right, Gillian?'

And I seem to remember saying something like, 'Kick. Head,' before my brain shut off.

The staff sprang into action. While someone rang for an ambulance, I was helped onto a seat where I felt a strange floating sensation; I was vaguely aware of what was going on around me but couldn't participate, and snippets of conversation drifted over me as I hovered in and out of consciousness.

Someone patted my arm and said, 'Don't go to sleep, you've got to stay awake, they'll be here soon.'

And they were. Someone kept a lookout for the ambulance and swung the entrance gates wide as soon as it was spotted hurtling up the lane towards the school. Out jumped the ambulance men, and within minutes they were immobilising my head and neck with one of those plastic supports, strapping an oxygen mask over my face, lifting me onto a stretcher and into the ambulance. On the way to the hospital, one of the chaps kept me chatting, or rather, he kept chatting, telling me not to go to sleep whilst I managed to mumble the odd word here and there, just to prove that some bits of my brain were actually functioning.

Meanwhile, amidst the tranquillity of the cliff tops, Mike's walk was unceremoniously interrupted by the shrill ringing of his mobile phone, just as his group were nearing one of the highlights of the walk: the lunchtime refreshment stop at a coastal pub of some repute.

In that 'no frills' way that horsey people have, one of the riding school staff said, 'Mike?'

'Yes?'

'Now don't get worried, Gillian's hit her head, but the ambulance is here now.'

'What! What happened?'

'She was kicked in the head by the horse, it was an accident.'

'Good God! Which hospital is she going to?'

'They've taken her to Queen's.'

'I'll be on my way as soon as I can get back to my car.'

'Can you let us know how she gets on, Mike?' the caller asked.

'Yes, as soon as I know what's happening I'll let you know. Bye.'

Unfortunately, Mike's car was parked at the starting point of their walk, some eight miles away, as was everyone else's. So he worked out that the quickest way to get back to the car was to continue walking for another couple of miles into the local village where he could get a train back to the previous town, then take a taxi from the station to his car. Having arrived at the nearest train station, Mike sat on the soulless railway platform munching on a south-eastern station sarnie, trying not to think about his lost repast and the culinary experience that all his colleagues were, by now, thoroughly enjoying.

The hospital staff were excellent. I was whisked through the triage in no time and transferred to a temporary bed in the casualty ward, smelly boots and all. The doctor was soon at my bedside, shining lights in my eyes and whatever else they do to assess possible damage.

'Kicked in the head by a horse, you say. Are you wearing any make-up?'

'No,' I responded, thinking to myself, that's a funny question.

But it was a good job I couldn't see what he could, because the thick, black blood lines of a bruise were already forming like kohl around my eye socket and eyelid. I expect stranger mistakes have been made, and not wishing to be caught out by the female tendency to smother an assortment of colours around their eyes, the doctor probably thought it wise to ask before making a diagnosis.

'We'll need X-rays and a scan on this one,' I heard the doctor call out, as he jotted down some notes on a clipboard and stuck it on the metal framework at the bottom of my bed.

By the time I was out of X-ray, Mike had arrived in casualty, looking somewhat harassed.

'Hello, darling,' he said. 'What on earth have you been up to now?'

'It wasn't her fault,' I said. 'Please don't blame Sadie, it wasn't her fault.'

'Oh darling,' Mike sighed.

We waited for the results, and Mike found a magazine to read at my bedside while he stroked my arm through the metal bedrail. By the time the results were back I felt a bit more compos mentis, but I had the mother of all headaches and could barely open my eyes.

'You were lucky,' the doctor said, 'we can't see any bone fractures on the X-rays or the scan, but you have got concussion and we'd like to keep an eye on you for a bit.'

'That's a relief,' Mike said. 'Will she have to stay in overnight, Doctor, or can she go home?' he added.

'We'll see how she is after a couple of hours. I'll come back and check her later on and let you know then.'

I dozed and Mike read, and when the doctor came back he asked me to tell him my name and address and date of birth and did I know why I was in hospital, and through the throbbing pain in my head I managed to answer all his questions. Then he placed his hand in front of my face and asked me to tell him how many fingers he was holding up. I said three and got it right, so then I said, 'Can we go home now, Doctor?'

And fortunately he said, 'Yes.' But I was to come back immediately if I felt sick or dizzy or became drowsy or floppy or the headache persisted. Mike dealt with the discharge papers while the nurse gave me something for my headache and we left the hospital, clutching a list of 'do's' and 'don'ts' following a head injury. An hour later we were home.

The following day my mum was drafted in on 'bed watch' as Mike didn't want to leave me alone while he went down to the supermarket for a fresh supply of pain killers. She gasped when she walked into the room.

'Oh, look at your poor face!' she cried.

Yes, I admit, I did look rather a mess. The bruise from the blow was really coming out now and a range of shades of blue, purple and black were spreading from my temple, across my eye and down my cheek. Very colourful.

'That horse is dangerous!' Mum continued in earnest.

'Don't be daft. It wasn't her fault,' I said, trying to explain the situation.

'But you could have lost your eye or been killed,' Mum added.

'That could happen while crossing the road, Mum. It was an accident;

she didn't do it on purpose. There was this fly and she didn't know my head was under her belly, it's a blind spot, you see…'

'Well, if you say so,' Mum said at the finish, sounding unconvinced.

'Go and put the kettle on, we'll have a cup of tea,' I said, changing the subject.

Mum got up from the chair by the bed and started towards the bedroom door when she stopped, half turned and gave me her parting shot, 'I've gone right off horses.'

Mike banned me from going to the yard until the doctor declared me fit.

'Oh, but why, honey?' I whinged. 'I'm only going to see Sadie; I'm not going to do any riding or anything.'

'I know you. You'll get carried away and say… I'll just get Sadie in… I'll just do this… I'll just do that…' he said, mimicking me in a high, squeaky voice.

'No, I won't,' I said, innocently.

'You won't be able to stop yourself,' he persisted. 'When the doctor says it's okay, then you can go, and not a day earlier!'

I knew deep down that he was right, so that was that, as they say. Instead I telephoned the yard and asked them if maybe one of the other girls could take Sadie out for a ride one day, not too far, maybe round the block or something.

A few days later I telephoned for an update. Someone had tried to take Sadie out for a short hack, but they didn't get very far. Whatever it was that poor Sadie saw, we'll never know, but she dug her heels in and remained firmly in reverse until her rider dismounted and led her back to the school.

'So we'll leave her out in the field until you're better, Gillian. We think that's the best thing to do.'

In a way I felt almost vindicated. Perhaps it wasn't me who was such a terrible rider after all, perhaps it was just Sadie being Sadie.

When I was finally firing on all cylinders and Mike felt he could let me loose on the world again, I went straight up to the yard to see Sadie. My goodness, she was looking well when I brought her in from the field –

a little too well, according to everyone else.

'She's getting fat,' the yard manager declared. 'She needs more exercise.'

So I made life easy for myself and took her into the cool of the indoor arena, set her loose and cracked the whip behind her. Off she went as I knew she would, shaking her neck, tail held high, and I marvelled, once again, at the miracle that had made her mine.

CHAPTER 24

N ow, I know I always said that I wasn't interested in dressage or technical horsemanship, but then I'd never owned a horse like Sadie. When she decided to behave, she radiated style and elegance in the arena, arching that graceful neck of hers and showing off her paces with panache.

The summer competition season was in full swing by now and the riding school owners suggested holding an in-house dressage competition for all their regular riders. This idea met with great excitement, and the proposed routines were split into classes according to the level of difficulty. A date was arranged, a judge hired for the afternoon and our instructor was suddenly inundated with requests for private dressage lessons. I couldn't help noticing some of the riders as they practised their routines and gradually I became infected by their enthusiasm. I decided that there was no reason why Sadie and I couldn't turn our hand to a spot of dressage. Okay, it would mean getting to grips with real riding technique, but there was a novice class planned and even if we made a mess of it we could have some fun trying. As the countdown began, we all took sneaky peaks at each other as we practised, trying to gauge who was doing the best and who might be in with a chance of winning a rosette.

'I don't mind entering, but I don't want to come last!' wailed one of the girls.

'Oh, go on. It's only a bit of fun, anyway,' I chided.

But secretly, I felt exactly the same. I knew we didn't have a hope in hell's chance of winning, but there was no way I wanted to come last. It may have started out as a 'bit of fun' but the competitive spirit soon bubbled to the surface and everyone, suddenly, was in earnest.

At higher level dressage the rider is expected to memorise the routine when competing, but the rules were more relaxed for our in-house competition and riders were allowed to have someone 'call' each step of the routine from the sidelines. I needed to rope in reinforcements to assist me and that meant Mike.

'Whatcha doing a week on Sunday?' I asked, innocently.

'Nothing much,' Mike replied, pausing for a second or two before adding suspiciously, '…why?'

'I need you to call my dressage routine, hon.'

'Can't you find somebody else to do it?' Mike squawked.

'No, I can't,' I wheedled, 'everyone else is either warming up, riding or preparing for the advanced class. I'll never be able to remember the routine and cope with Sadie at the same time. Mike, I need you… please call my routine for me…?'

'Oh… all right,' Mike said reluctantly. 'You'll have to tell me exactly what to do, and *don't blame me* if it all goes wrong! Do you hear?'

'Of course, dear,' I said, all sweetness and light – and having press-ganged Mike to be my caller, I presented him with my dressage sheet.

'What does this mean? It's all gobbledegook to me,' he said, stunned.

'I'll explain it all to you. Really… it's easy, honey. Just be aware that you need to read out the next step *before* I finish the previous one, so I know where I'm going,' I said. 'Look, we'll do a "dry run" in the garden, give you a bit of practice.'

Mike scratched his head. So we decamped to our back garden for Mike to get the gist of calling a change of direction, whilst I jogged circles and turns across the lawn.

It was a good job the neighbours weren't about because I don't know what they'd've made of me prancing in a half-circle as Mike directed me to 'Turn on the forehand' and proceed 'Down the centreline at "C"'. I soon discovered that Mike's attention span for calling out dressage routines was fairly limited, so to add some authenticity to our rehearsal, we adjourned to the riding school to practise the real thing.

It was during one of these sessions that I heard through the horsey grapevine about a second-hand dressage saddle. It was up for sale because the owner's horse had outgrown it and I spied it on show in the tack room. It looked rather posh sitting there waiting for a buyer, with its straight-cut saddle flaps, deep seat and big knee rolls.

'Might fit your Sadie,' someone said in passing, and my ears pricked up.

'How much are they asking for it?' I flung casually into the conversation.

'Don't know, but it's bound to be reasonable – half the price at least of a new one. Why not give it a try; see if it fits?'

Why not, I thought. I gave the saddle fitter a ring and a few days later they called at the yard to check the saddle on Sadie.

Feeling almost like a pro now, I handed over my girth, saying confidently, 'I know that the saddle is being sold without a girth, so I've taken this one from my other saddle.'

The response soon put me in my place.

'But that's a general purpose girth; it's no good for this saddle. It's too long. You'll need a dressage girth for this.'

And there was me, thinking that I actually knew what I was talking about.

We borrowed another girth from the riding school, and Sadie stood quietly while the saddler got cracking.

'Yes, it's not a bad fit. But the flocking needs to be adjusted, here...' she pointed, '...and here, in the panels underneath.'

Flocking is the stuffing that goes into a saddle, and it can make an amazing difference to the fit and comfort of the saddle for both horse and rider.

'How long will it take to do the flocking?' I asked.

'Oh, I can do it on site for you now, if you want to buy the saddle,' she replied.

I didn't have to think about it very long, all of two seconds probably. I was hooked and, half an hour later, became the proud owner of a dressage saddle. The only thing was, I didn't realise that I would also need a new saddle cloth. It wasn't until I noticed that my old one was all concertinaed up underneath the dressage saddle that I knew I'd have to go back to the shops again.

I chose a royal blue saddle cloth, to match the blue brushing boots that Sadie already had, and was trying it on at the yard when someone said, 'Is that for the competition?'

I nodded.

'But it's not white.'

'White? Why should it be white?'

'Because white is the standard colour for dressage competitions.'

'No one mentioned anything to me about competition cloths having to be white. And anyway, I chose royal blue to match her boots,' I added by way of explanation.

'Not allowed them either, in a dressage competition.'

Dear me. White saddle cloths, no brushing boots, would I never learn…?

Exasperated, I made another trip back to the shops and exchanged the blue saddle cloth for a white one, making sure that I had finally bought the right one this time.

Dressage Day loomed ever closer and someone at the yard said, 'Of course you'll have to get Sadie all plaited up for the competition.'

'Plaited… yes, of course,' I said, wondering who I could coerce into showing me how to plait a mane and tail. But as soon as I mentioned it, I found that I wasn't the only one who needed the practice, so our instructor agreed to show us how it should be done.

First, the mane – which had to be trimmed if it was too long – was parted into small equal sections. Each section was then plaited, secured with a tiny rubber band, rolled under and secured again. Sound easy? It's not. The only way I could see to do the job properly was to stand on a box. And it was from those dizzying heights that I needed to hold the comb, plait the section (needed both hands for that, so comb went in waistband), fix a tiny rubber band on the end of the plait, without letting go (this is where a third hand would be useful…), then roll up plait, need two hands again for this, get another tiny elastic band ready… See what I mean?

Plaiting the tail was worse than the mane – but at least I was standing on terra firma to do the job. Sadie's time was spent far more productively than mine that afternoon, as she stoically munched her way through a full hay net and a bag of carrots, whilst I huffed and puffed the hours away, getting nowhere fast.

Unfortunately, the only plaiting bands at the school were black and I needed white ones for Sadie, so that meant another unscheduled stop on my way home. Funny how these little shopping trips never seem to get mentioned when Mike arrives home…

Dressage Day finally dawned. I piled all my gear into the car, clean white jodhpurs, white top, black jacket, freshly polished boots, some make-up and a hair net that I'd borrowed from my mum the previous evening, and set off for the school. There was a real buzz of excitement on the yard that day, as we bathed our horses, trimmed up any wispy bits of hair that spoilt their outline, polished their feet and plaited their manes and tails.

Towards lunchtime I started to panic, thinking I'd never get the plaits finished in time, when a friend stepped in and lent a hand to finish the job.

We had lots of visitors on the yard: parents, friends and relatives, who all came to cheer on the competitors and admire the horses, with their glossy coats and gleaming tack that sparkled and shone in the sunshine.

Dressed up to the nines in her plaits and shoe shine, Sadie looked really smart and I was tying her up on the yard when I heard a child's voice say, 'Oh, look at that horse! It's got PINK SPOTS!'

Nobody really paid any attention to her, but she took a few steps closer to me, pointed at Sadie and repeated with conviction, 'That white horse has got pink spots.'

I looked at Sadie again and suddenly it dawned on me – she was talking about the tiny flecks of colour in Sadie's coat. I moved closer and peered at her coat. The child was absolutely right; those random flecks were quite pink in the afternoon sunlight. I'd never thought of them as pink before.

'Yes,' I replied with a smile. 'She *has* got pink spots, hasn't she?

The child nodded. 'Is that your horse?'

'Yes, she's mine,' I said. 'She's called Sadie, and you can stroke her if you want to.'

Her small hand reached out, and with one finger she gently traced the 'pink' spots on Sadie's shoulder until someone called her name and she skipped off to rejoin her family.

Shortly before we were due to start warming up, Mike arrived and inspected Sadie while I changed into my clean riding gear.

'Everything going to plan?' he asked.

'Yeh, just about ready, hon,' I said. 'Bit nervous though, don't know why – it's supposed to be fun…' I said apprehensively.

'Oh, come on,' said Mike, putting it into perspective, 'you'll be all right once you get going, just enjoy yourself.'

He gave me a big smile as he spoke, and because smiles are infectious, I smiled back.

Despite being on the windy side, the weather held for us. Once we were in the arena and the klaxon sounded for the start of our routine, I was too busy concentrating to notice anything else. Sadie wasn't impressed with all the rigmarole of participation, which made my job much harder, and as Mike called out the turns and changes of gait, I felt the sweat prick my back underneath the cool exterior of my jacket. But we managed to complete the course without incident or embarrassment and I was reasonably satisfied with the outcome.

After the last entry had taken place, we all waited with baited breath for our score sheets and those with the highest were duly announced as winners. Sadie and I were placed in the middle of our class, and whilst we didn't win a rosette, we didn't come last. For a first attempt – I didn't think we did too badly.

When Sadie was ready for the field, I led her out through the gate and mulled over the day as we walked down the lane. Some of the girls were positively put out that Sadie didn't put on a show like she had at the Christmas jump-off, and when I looked back to those first months together, I thought how far we had actually come from those beleaguered beginnings. Then I turned my head and noticed the farmer's land to the side of us; that self-same field that Sadie had fled across all those months ago. How things had changed. Now, that field was no longer a great swathe of muddy troughs, but filled with young green corn slowly ripening in the sun. Their long, slender stalks rustled harmoniously as they bowed to the gentle breeze that blew them in undulating waves over the land, like an ocean swell across the sea. And in some ways, I thought, that corn was a lot like me and Sadie. Our friendship too had slowly ripened and our confidence in each other had grown just like that field of corn, imperceptibly at first, but stronger now. Instead of eyeing each other up warily, afraid that our fragile beginnings would be crushed in a moment of misunderstanding, we had found trust and harmony together, enabling us to bend with the moving tide of existence, instead of being broken by circumstance and the inevitability of life.

Driving home that day, my mind wandered to someone else who was also going home – the little girl I'd seen at the riding school. I imagined her running in to the rest of her family, telling them about the pretty horse she had seen, and I smiled to myself. How would her family react to the news of a white horse with pink spots? Probably put it down to a young child's vivid imagination, when all the time it was perfectly true. Out of the mouths of babes and children, don't they say?

CHAPTER 25

With the furore of the competition all over and done with, it was back to business on the yard and time for the scrutiny. When I arrived for my next lesson, the instructor asked, 'Have you got your dressage score sheet?'

'Yep,' I replied, waving the flimsy sheet of paper in the air. 'Got it here.'

'Let's have a look then,' she said without preamble, and we pored over the marks with their accompanying comments, noting where I'd done well, where there was room for improvement and where there'd been a disaster or two.

Spurred on by the judges' comments, I was convinced that we could do much better, so I decided to work harder on my position and Sadie's attentiveness. My first port of call was the shops (mind you, I never seemed to be out of them these days…), to buy a schooling whip. This is longer than the ordinary crop and enabled me to reach right across to Sadie's bottom with a flick of my wrist. Perfect! The new whip made its grand entrance at our next private lesson, where both Sadie and I were put through our paces in earnest.

Somehow it seemed that the more I learnt about riding, the more I realised how little I knew and how much more there was to discover. For instance, I had never realised how incredibly sensitive horses are to their riders; even a small imbalance in the rider's position can affect a horse's performance.

I found out from my instructor that I have a tendency to lean to one side; yet when she mentioned it, I thought I was sitting up straight.

This sort of detail isn't so much of a problem if you are just hacking out in the countryside, but it makes an enormous difference if you are hoping to learn to jump, perform dressage or compete at shows, because of the impact that both rhythm and balance have on performance. Like humans, horses can also favour one side over the other and a good rider can help their horse redress the balance, which is why it is important to work them equally on their left and right sides.

Horses are incredibly perceptive and have the ability to pick up on their rider's thoughts and feelings. This was brought home to me during a lesson when some poles from an earlier jumping session were neatly stacked in the corner of the indoor arena. On the first circuit, Sadie spooked a little as we rode past them – nothing too naughty, just a twitch to the side, which I tried to ignore. Second time around, I thought that Sadie would be better, but she wasn't. Every time we rode past those poles, she skedaddled to one side.

Suddenly my instructor said to me, 'Are you looking at those poles in the corner?'

'Yes, I am,' I said. 'Gotta keep my eye on them because Sadie will spook when we ride by 'em.'

'Well, don't, because that's part of the problem,' she replied. 'Sadie is picking up on the fact that you are looking at them. Even if she's not scared of something, if you keep looking at it, she'll think that there *is* something to be frightened of.'

'How does she know what I'm looking at?' I said in amazement.

'From your body language. When you are nervous, your muscles tighten up and she'll feel that. She'll feel it through your hands, your grip on the reins or your seat, which will tense in the saddle. So try looking past those poles and focus on the side that you're riding towards.'

I may have been sceptical at first, but the next time I made a concerted effort to look straight ahead, past the corner and on to the next point in the circle that we were moving towards. And do you know what? We sailed straight past those poles in the corner without a hitch. Amazing! Who would have thought that something as simple as looking past an obstacle, instead of directly at it, would have made such a difference?

When we came out of the lesson, both of us were hot and I headed straight for the hosepipe. I rinsed the sweat off Sadie, and while I waited for her to dry I turned the hose on myself. I splashed my face and watched the cooling rivulets of water as they ran down my forearm, forging their way around the tiny blonde hairs that pricked my skin, taking the path of least resistance, yet arriving at the same destination regardless. I thought too about what I had learnt in the lesson and then it struck me. Had I made the same mistake in my own life? Had I concentrated too intently on an obstacle, rather than the objective? Problems would always exist; we couldn't avoid them. But perhaps I could minimise their impact by changing my perspective and focusing on the greater picture beyond.

CHAPTER 26

All of a sudden it was October; spring and summer had run head-long into autumn and the anniversary of Sadie's purchase. A year! I couldn't believe that I'd had Sadie for a year. Time can play such tricks on us. On the one hand it seemed like only yesterday that I'd sat in my car with mounting anticipation as I waited for Sadie to arrive; but then again, I couldn't remember a day when Sadie hadn't been part of my life. My daily routine was now unrecognisable from a year ago; muddy boots were a permanent feature in our hallway, numerous cupboards had become designated for riding gear only, carrots and apples were noted on the shopping list as 'ours' and 'horse', a separate dirty washing basket for horsey apparel had appeared and bits of stable bedding seemed to perme-ate our bungalow. With limited storage space at the riding school not even our garage had escaped unscathed, with metal mouseproof bins to keep feed in on one side and laundered horse coats, labelled and stacked on the other.

Then there was the inevitable junk mail. It's quite amazing how quickly retailers discover that you are a horse owner, and suddenly you're on eve-rybody's mailing list. Flyers and leaflets, advertising everything from the latest equine vitamin supplements to magazine subscriptions, came pouring through the letter box with alarming alacrity. Not to mention the vet-erinary reminders for worming and vaccinations that needed to be sifted from the discard pile before everything disappeared into the recycling sack together.

And what of my illness, how had I managed? All through those months my colitis had lurked in the background, persistently rumbling on like an amoebic parasite, tenacious and ever present, sapping my energy like the bloodsucker it was. Was Sadie able to restore my health? Was she the miracle cure I longed for?

In a nutshell, no. But that depends on what is meant by a 'cure'. Rarely is anything as clear-cut as black and white, more a matter of varying degrees of grey, particularly in the medical profession.

I had always considered myself to be reasonably fit and healthy; I enjoyed sport at school and into adulthood I tried to keep pace with various fitness trends as they came and went. When jogging became all the rage, I was there on the streets with the rest of them, all kitted out in my shiny shell suit, arguably one of the biggest fashion faux pas ever to hit the high street. But it wasn't long before the lonely pounding of pavements in inclement weather lost its appeal and the advent of the aerobics video that could be pursued in the comfort of my own home became a much more attractive option. Alongside all of this physical activity I also had a healthy appetite. I could polish off a large plate of chips, with nothing more than a hiccup to come from my thin and wiry frame. Despite being bludgeoned by this cascade of calories, my body remained staunchly impervious to the added pounds that others seemed to gain, resulting in my firm belief that metabolism and genes are the ultimate adjudicators in the battle of the bulge. But even these building blocks of humanity failed to overcome the devastation wrought by my colitis, where my appetite floundered, my strength failed and my angular cheekbones disappeared beneath a bloated exterior caused by a surfeit of steroid medication. Against what seemed to be almost insurmountable odds, I lost my enthusiasm to carry on. When I wasn't in bed, I clung to our house like a shipwrecked mariner to flotsam, and the thought of going anywhere without immediate access to a toilet was enough to set off a panic attack.

But Sadie took me out of the bubble of despair that separated me from the rest of the world and she gave me back my focus. She motivated me, when nothing else did. When a flare-up of colitis confined me to bed, it wasn't my job or the minutiae of everyday living that I longed to get better for; it was to ride. I yearned to sit on my horse again, feel the freedom of a canter and forget how dysfunctional my inadequate body had become.

However well meaning people are, it can be very difficult for them to relate to someone with a chronic illness. In my experience, their reactions tend to vary from being sorry, to pity and, sometimes, sheer relief that they don't have it themselves – and who can blame them?

But animals aren't like this; they relate to people on a completely different level and that's what makes them so important to their owners. Sadie didn't need to look past my illness to see me; my illness didn't exist in her eyes. I was just a 'normal' human being to her; one that cared for her, fed her and never betrayed her trust. When I turned up to see her every day, she didn't ask me if I was feeling okay, whether I was having a good day or a bad day, neither did she chide me for being too early, too late or too slow, she simply accepted me.

So often I think we are unintentionally categorised by those who love us. We become the mother, the wife, the sister, the daughter, boxed in by those parameters and unseen for the person that we are. Even friendships can be hurtful and ambiguous. But there is no guile in a dog that greets its owner with exuberance and joy; the owner never pauses to consider if this display of affection hides another truth. And it is this transparency, unshakeable trust and complete acceptance of who we are that makes the interaction between humans and animals so compelling and the bond so powerful.

For my part, I mucked out Sadie's stable, pushed heavy wheelbarrows piled high with dung over to the muck heap, carried buckets of water backwards and forwards, lifted bales of wood shavings and bags of feed in and out of my car, and where my muscles had been wasted by high doses of steroids, my arms and legs would ache with exertion. I would huff and puff in an effort to catch my breath, whilst I leant, out of sight, against the stable wall, thinking, I'm too old for all this!

But, gradually, my strength returned and I became more confident about tackling a variety of tasks that I would never have dreamt of doing two years ago. For the first time since my diagnosis I *did* feel on a par with all the other girls on the yard. I was just another livery girl who loved her horse to bits, and it was Sadie who put me there.

No, she didn't cure me, I still have an ongoing battle with my colitis, but most of the time I no longer feel held to ransom by it. I've looked it straight in the eye and tried to get on with my life, and when I've had a good couple of months, I do feel almost 'cured'. And, who knows, maybe one day that word remission might also apply to me, and if it does I know that a lot of the credit must surely go to Sadie.

CHAPTER 27

If I hadn't been daydreaming that morning as I walked Sadie in from the field, I probably would have noticed it sooner. But as it was, I sauntered along the lane without a care in the world and only noticed it when I started to clean the mud out of her feet. With my hoof pick at the ready, I picked up Sadie's back leg and then I saw it. I couldn't believe my eyes – her iron horseshoe had somehow twisted itself round to one side of her hoof and was jutting out about half an inch on the inside of her foot.

How had she managed to do that? I couldn't imagine what she'd been doing up at the field to twist her shoe in such a way. But… thinking on… I had seen her careening across the field, flat out at a gallop with the wind up her tail, so maybe I shouldn't have been so surprised.

My dilemma, however, was what should I do with the bent shoe? I couldn't leave it as it was because Sadie could easily injure her other hind leg if she caught it on the twisted metal jutting out from her foot. So I decided that my only option was to remove the shoe completely, thinking, how hard can that be? I noticed a couple of the nails were already missing and if Sadie could move the shoe that far off centre, then I should be able to complete the job in no time at all; the farrier would be here in a couple of days for his weekly visit and he could replace it then. I soon found out that this was easier said than done. Bending over at an awkward angle, I huffed and puffed but I could not get that shoe to budge – it was jammed into position, even though there seemed to be nothing of substance holding it in place. I needed someone with a bit more strength than I could muster, that's for sure, so I recruited one of the riding school staff who'd had some previous experience with badly behaving horseshoes and was willing to lend a hand.

'I can't shift this bloomin' shoe,' I said. 'Look at the state of it!' I lifted Sadie's hind leg and we both peered at the offending article.

'You'll never get the shoe off like that,' I was told in no uncertain terms. 'You need something like a pair of pliers to grip it with.'

This request produced a lot of rummaging around in car boots and tool kits and someone soon produced a likely contender. Armed with the pliers, my accomplice set to work. After a considerable amount of effort and more than a few expletives, the rogue shoe finally bounced off onto the concrete with a resounding clang and the job was done.

It seemed strange walking back to the field along the tarmacadam lane, where the usual rhythmical four-stroke tempo of Sadie's walk had changed to an eerie one, two, three... hush... as if someone was hitting the pause button every fourth step, and the errant shoe proclaimed its absence in the silence of the missing beat.

CHAPTER 28

Winter can be hard on the yard, especially for the girls that work at the riding school. For the most part we had been lucky that year; autumn had mellowed into mild wintery days and we were all hoping that the season of good cheer would be kind to us. But when a cold front shouldered its way onto the scene, the temperatures plummeted and the biting cold numbed your fingers almost as soon as you stepped out of the car. Suddenly thermal underwear became de rigueur and the only way to keep warm was to keep working. It certainly gave me a new respect for all those people whose work dictated they spend most of their time outdoors, all year round, braving whatever the weather threw at them.

But I think the hardest days were those when the icy temperatures grabbed the yard's water pipes in a stranglehold and froze the lot. Like any animal, horses cannot survive without water and even in the winter they need copious amounts to digest their feed and hay. On these days, the only supply of running water to be found was from the taps in the yard owner's house. Buckets, jerry cans and any other available receptacle had to be filled to the brim and carried backwards and forwards to the horses' stables to keep them watered.

Fortunately for me, the grazing field where Sadie was turned out was large enough to accommodate horses on a year-round basis. If it had been any smaller, the horses' hooves would have turned the ground into a quagmire during the wet weather, destroying the delicate new blades of grass as they pushed their way through the earth in early spring. More time in the field meant less mucking out of a dirty stable and a better exercise regime for Sadie, so I kept her turned out on all but the coldest of days. I made sure that she was well rugged up with winter coats, ignoring the comments about Sadie's knees buckling under the weight of her duvets, as I thrust my hand between the rugs and the toasty warmth of her skin to check her temperature. The livery yard kept a check on the quantity of grazing, supplementing poor-quality grass with extra bales of haylage, which were transported on the massive arms of farm tractors and deposited into metal feed bins in the middle of the field.

There was no room for complacency, however, and although we didn't ride so often in the cold, wintery months, I would bring Sadie back to the yard for routine grooming and general health checks. I would inspect her feet, look for cuts and grazes and make sure that her rugs fitted properly and remained waterproof. Much to Mike's relief, it was during these months that my car really came into its own; safely carrying me along foggy streets, across flooded roads and down icy lanes, with no hint of the computer malfunction it had suffered so early on in its new life with us.

One winter's day when I brought Sadie in from the field, I noticed a small sore on her chest, where the buckle of her rug was fastened. Although Sadie had been wearing this same rug for several months without a problem, it was clear that the small bald patch had been created by the metal fastening rubbing her chest as she stretched out her neck to graze. This sort of thing can easily cause an abscess if it isn't dealt with promptly, and I definitely didn't want any painful blisters or unnecessary vet's fees if I could help it. A quick decision was needed if Sadie was to go back to the field that day, and the only way to be absolutely sure that the sore patch wouldn't be exacerbated any further was to buy a replacement rug. Two hours later I was back on the yard with a new one that had a larger overlap at the front and an off-centre buckle fastening, instead of an interlocking clip. When I checked on Sadie a few days later, our suspicions about the old rug proved to be correct; the sore spot had healed over and soft, downy hair was already beginning to reappear around it.

I hated this cold weather, and once the furore of Christmas and the New Year were all over and done with, I had a tendency to mark time as I waited for the first signs of spring to touch the land and bring me out of my winter stupor. Valentine's Day fell on a Saturday this year, and when Mike suggested a naughty weekend away somewhere to break the gloom of winter, I was all for it.

The night before we left, I crammed a posh frock, high heels and new undies into an overnight bag, and the following morning Mike whisked me off to Poole for our romantic weekend. Pricewise, Mike had pushed the boat out. He'd chosen an elegant Victorian guest house which was tucked away in a quiet suburban cul-de-sac, next to the sea front. On arrival we were taken upstairs to our suite, which was decorated in antique style with a magnificent four-poster bed bedecked with brocade and an en suite Victorian bathroom complete with free-standing, roll-topped bath and gold taps. There was a comfy sitting area in front of a curved bay window with stunning sea views across the bay; and tucked away in an alcove was a small, but fully functional, kitchenette. It was lovely. As soon as Mike closed the door, I did a back flip onto the bed with my arms outstretched and bounced on the covers. Two seconds later he joined me and we giggled like teenagers enjoying an illicit romp.

Valentine's Day dawned bright and clear but we remained deep under the covers of that sumptuous bed until we were roused from our reverie by the discreet knock of our hostess, telling us she had left our breakfast on trays outside our room. Mike did the decent thing and slid out of bed to bring them in before our coffee went cold. Propped up on pillows, we tucked into a 'full English' and opened our cards to each other.

We had been together as a couple for quite a few years now, and whilst I hoped to get married one day, Mike had already been on that merry-go-round once and it had left a bitter aftertaste in his mouth. In a way, I too was protective of my single status, enjoying that contradictory mix of retaining my independence whilst sharing my life with a permanent partner. We loved each other and were happy together, so it wasn't an issue that either of us had dwelt on.

Then a funny thing happened. Before he'd finished his coffee, Mike suddenly started fumbling around in a jacket pocket and knelt down on one knee by the bed. I thought he'd dropped a teaspoon, but no! He whipped out a small box and proudly opened the lid to reveal the most gorgeous sapphire and diamond ring ensconced on a bed of dark blue velvet.

'Marry me, Gill?' he said.

My initial reaction was shock, I had no idea that Mike was planning to propose, but I soon found my voice. How could I refuse?

'Oh, it's beautiful, Mike,' I said as I plucked the ring from its velvet niche.

Mike had done his research and the ring was a perfect fit as he slipped it onto my finger and gave me a big hug. I spent the rest of the day sneaking furtive glances at the unfamiliar addition – extending my hand at arm's length and flexing my fingers to check out the sparkle as the stones caught the light; the ring felt big and heavy on my finger, symbolic of our commitment and a reminder that I was now officially engaged.

As soon as we arrived home, the first person I called was my mum.

'Hello, it's me,' I said excitedly.

'Oh hello, darling. Did you have a nice weekend in Poole?' she asked.

'Yes, we did, we had a really fantastic time. I was just phoning to see if you were going to be in this afternoon, because Mike and I wanted to pop round. We've got some "news" for you!' I said, wanting to keep her on tenterhooks without giving the game away.

'Oh, well then,' she replied. 'If that's the case, you'd better come round now.'

When we arrived at my mum's, she opened the door expectantly. I waved my hands around in a rather exaggerated fashion, hoping that she would spot the ring straight off, but I'm afraid she didn't take the bait and in the end I couldn't stand the suspense.

'Mike's asked me to marry him,' I gushed, 'we're engaged, look at my beautiful ring.'

'Oh,' she said, sounding almost disappointed. 'I thought you were going to say you were pregnant…'

Crickey, I thought, considering I was heading into my fifties, Mum was really pushing her luck with that one.

CHAPTER 29

The day started off like any other. My time was my own and I took a slow stroll along the lane to the field. Would she be a good girl to catch today, I wondered, or would she race around like crazy giving me a hard time? Sadie was fairly close to the gate when I arrived and she looked me straight in the eye without moving. She waited placidly while I put her headcollar on, and with a minimal amount of coaxing, she followed me slowly back to the stable. It did cross my mind that Sadie was surprisingly sedate today, but I really thought nothing of it on the short walk back to the yard.

Just as I was tying her up, a colleague, who was standing behind us, glanced across and called out, 'What's wrong with Sadie's back leg?'

I looked round quickly and gasped, 'Oh my goodness!'

Sadie's leg, around the joint called the hock, was swollen to about twice its normal size. I gently ran my hand over the swelling; it was hot to the touch, indicating inflammation, although there were no signs of a cut or puncture wound.

No discussion was needed to reach the conclusion that this was most definitely a job for the vet. I phoned our local vet, explained the situation and he agreed to call in at the yard later that morning. When he arrived he asked me to walk Sadie up and down to assess how lame she was and then gently prodded the area around the swollen joint with his fingertips. The diagnosis was narrowed down to a suspected pulled ligament, and Sadie was prescribed a course of anti-inflammatories and a period of box rest.

I had never heard the term 'box rest' before, which literally means that the horse must remain confined to her stable box to rest the leg, allowing it to heal, but the process was to become so frustrating and protracted that the mere mention of those words now makes my blood run cold. The problem with horses is that you can't reason with them and you can't explain to them that they need a programme of rest and gradual rehabilitation when a tendon or ligament is damaged. Neither do they understand that a newly mended ligament needs a gentle reintroduction to exercise otherwise it will just tear again, requiring even longer to heal second time around. As soon as horses start to feel better, they naturally want to release all their pent-up energy, so it is up to the owner to carefully manage their return to fitness in a controlled environment – starting with a few minutes at walk on a lead rein, before gradually increasing the amount of exercise over the following weeks. Even the smallest mistake, like trotting too soon, can be enough to set back the healing process by weeks.

So, I had my orders and poor Sadie was restricted to quarters. Some horses can really fret when they are put on box rest and become so restless that they need to be sedated. Fortunately Sadie took it all in her stride and seemed to accept her confinement with equanimity. Mind you, she did have a comfy stable to sleep in and her appetite never missed a beat. She loved her food and I always made sure she had a good supply of carrots.

Every day I expected to see some improvement, but each time I checked on Sadie the hock looked just as swollen as it had the previous day. The days dragged by and I became concerned about her lack of progress. Was the diagnosis right? Was there any other type of treatment? I just didn't know. Yet again friends and acquaintances stepped in – just like mothers giving advice on past experiences with their own 'children' – and suggestions from the horse fraternity came thick and fast. After ten days with no improvement, I decided to ask for a second opinion from an equine vet who was more specialised in dealing with horse injuries. I gave a brief explanation of Sadie's diagnosis over the phone and vet no. 2 agreed to call at the yard the following day on his rounds, but couldn't be more specific than a 'sometime after lunch' approximation, as all manner of complications can bubble to the surface during routine appointments.

It was another dull and rainy day, and after what seemed like an interminable wait the vet arrived at the yard. I fussed and worried and tried to stay calm for Sadie's sake, so that she wouldn't pick up on my anxiety and become difficult to manage. But when the vet examined Sadie he was relaxed and confident with an excellent 'bedside' manner (honed over the years, I suspect, to mitigate the effects of tearful, stressed-out owners who were more in need of his quiet bedside manner than ever any of his real patients were).

The verdict was an open one, with a range of possibilities, but the course of action was to have an ultrasound and X-ray the leg so that a definitive diagnosis could be made. However, this involved taking Sadie to the equine medical centre where the equipment was located and another problem reared its ugly head – transport. I didn't have any. But I needn't have worried. Friends rallied round yet again and our local farm shop, bless them, volunteered their time and their horse trailer to transport Sadie for her diagnostic tests.

There was a sharp intake of breath from Mike when I told him that Sadie needed to go to an equine medical centre for tests, as costs were spiralling. But this is where my insurance company stepped in and saved the day, and I am forever grateful for all the advice and assistance that I received from them – in particular how straightforward and prompt their claims process was. I had been so worried about Sadie that to have the financial burden of her injury taken care of was worth more to me than I can ever express.

Travel boots and tail guard, relegated to the 'B' list as non-essentials at the time of my horse purchase, suddenly sprung to the top of the shopping list and a quick trip to the shops had to be fitted in to rectify this. No point in taking her in the trailer if she was going to damage something else on the way. Appointments were confirmed and we were ready to go.

'Don't know what time I'll be home tonight, honey,' I called to Mike as I ran out of the front door, sandwich in hand. Mike's goodbye wave was coupled with an air of resignation that he had somehow become today's nominee for cooking the evening meal.

On arrival at the medical centre Sadie was reasonably cooperative, went easily into her allocated stall and was soon sedated. All the necessary gear was wheeled into her compartment and a series of X-rays were taken, followed by an ultrasound of the whole area. While Sadie was left to recover from the anaesthetic, I followed the vet into another section of the centre where the X-rays were developed and he explained his findings.

The news was not good. The ligament in her hock had been torn quite badly, but to compound matters, the X-ray had shown that Sadie also had a bone spavin in the hock. The vet explained that a spavin is a bony growth in the hock joint caused by osteoarthritis, which in itself is enough to cause lameness in a horse. He confirmed that I was doing all the right things for Sadie, but that she would need a protracted spell of box rest to allow the ligament to heal with only a brief spell of walking in hand (using a lead rope) each day. Most of the medical information I found difficult to digest, but what I did understand from it all was that there would be no quick fix for Sadie, both her and I were in this for the long run.

All that remained was to load Sadie back into the trailer and take her home. By this time, however, she was well cheesed off and showed her disapproval of the whole chain of events by refusing to re-enter the trailer. She spun round on the end of the rope like a whirling dervish every time we got her close to the bottom of the ramp, and I winced when I thought of the additional strain her recalcitrance might cause to that ligament. Herbal treats and carrots held no sway for her, and in the end we had to seek further assistance. With one of us on the front end and two pair of hands straining at the rear, we finally managed to get Sadie loaded after a lengthy tug of war.

Sweaty and breathless we jumped into the towing vehicle and pulled out of the medical centre to the vet's parting comment of, 'It's surprising how agile she is on that back leg of hers, considering all the damage to the hock.'

Indeed!

CHAPTER 30

B ack on the yard I visited Sadie every day and we fell into a daily routine, starting with her grooming, then her exercise and finishing up with her medication. I'm sure she anticipated my arrival because as soon as I turned the corner to her stable she would stretch her neck out towards me over her stable door, turning her head to the side and pursing her lips, almost as if she was blowing kisses at me. She was so endearing, so vulnerable, so reliant; she pulled at my heart strings and there was nothing I wouldn't do for her.

Yet despite having such an apparently simple regime, we soon ran into difficulties. The first problem on the agenda was Sadie's 'exercise', where we were supposed to have what was laughingly called five minutes of medium-paced walking in hand. We would normally start off okay, at least, for the first few yards, and then matters would quickly degenerate into a battle of wills between horse and handler. Using any old excuse, a breath of wind or a fluttering leaf, Sadie would break out into a funny sort of jig, similar to a type of on-the-spot trot as she went along, whilst I tried valiantly to keep her at a walk. I upped the ante by wearing suede gloves, which gave me a better grip on the lead rope, and I would dig my heels in as we walked and brace myself against her front shoulder to counteract her pushing forward. This became a great game for Sadie. Every day we would go through this fiasco, each trying to outwit the other and neither of us sure who would be the day's winner. Following her 'exercise' Sadie would retire to her stable and scoff for England. This necessitated a drastic cutback in her hard feed (a tasty mix of alfalfa and other goodies), and she was consequently relegated to a simple diet of hay – anything else would have had her out of her stable like Concorde off a runway.

However, in an effort to mitigate the effects of too much feed, we soon ran into a problem on the medication front. Now that Sadie's feed had been cut and she was only eating hay, I had to find a way of getting her to take the prescribed anti-inflammatories, which came in powder form in sachets.

No problem, I thought, I'll check out the local feed suppliers. I bought some chaff, sweetened with molasses (thinking that would disguise the taste), mixed a handful in a bucket with some carrots, added the anti-inflammatory powder and hey presto, good enough to fool the best, I said to myself. I took the bucket round to Sadie and she dived straight in… and straight out, snorting through her nostrils with such a look of disdain, as if her delicate sense of smell had just exposed an outrage. I tried to get her to eat some of it by stuffing the chaff into the side of her mouth, but she was having none of it. As fast as I stuffed it in one side, she spat it out of the other. I then tried coating just the carrots in the powder and initially I managed to get her to eat a few pieces, but her efforts were half-hearted and she soon decided she'd had enough. To press home the point, she turned her nose as far away from the proffered titbit as she could possibly get, twisting her neck round in the opposite direction like a contortionist. I became desperate to find a way to get Sadie to take her medication – so it was back to the drawing board.

I experimented with several different concoctions, including one using honey, but that girl's nose told her every time that someone had tampered with her food. I racked my brains for a solution, and then it came to me, an idea that couldn't possibly fail…

I hatched my plan, fine-tuned the detail and set off to the supermarket. I bought a special bag of kids' apples, which were small enough for Sadie to eat whole, and an apple corer. Back home I retreated to the kitchen and assembled my ingredients.

'Whatcha up to, honey?' Mike asked as he came in and surveyed the worktop strewn with apple cores and my back hunched forward over the sink.

'Apple pie?' he added with hopeful expectation.

'Gonna fix that crafty Sadie-bobs once and for all,' I said, my brow furrowed in concentration as I purposefully skewered another apple, carefully taking out the core without breaking the fruit into pieces.

'Sadie-bobs?' Mike queried in a baffled tone. 'What's she got to do with all this kitchen activity?'

By way of explanation, I pointed to the row of de-cored apples standing on the worktop like oversized Polo mints and said to Mike, 'You see, I'm going to use a piece of the core to put a "stopper" in the bottom end of the apple, tip the powder into the empty centre where I've removed the core and bung up the top with another piece of apple to keep the powder in. Then when I offer her the apple, she will eat it whole, and the anti-inflammatory will go down her gullet with the rest of the apple. What do you make of that idea, then?' I expounded.

'Very interesting...' came the sceptical response. 'Do you think she'll go for it?'

'Pretty foolproof if you ask me,' I said confidently. 'Just don't eat the apples from the fridge labelled "Sadie",' I added, as I wrote over the bag in thick black marker pen – the last thing I needed right now was a trip to the hospital with Mike suffering from an overdose of horse jollop.

Back at the yard the next day, I strode jauntily over to Sadie, apple in hand, and presented her with my fait accompli. That shiny little red morsel remained on my outstretched hand for all of two seconds before it disappeared into the depths of Sadie's cakehole. Yes! I punched the air in triumph, as I heard a great crunch from those pearly whites biting deep into my doctored apple. But my cry of success soon turned to disbelief when, a second later, a shower of apple chunks and globules of white foam sprayed from Sadie's mouth, hitting me squarely in the solar plexus before bouncing onto the concrete, as she spat out the lot.

In the end, I found a much simpler way of giving Sadie her medicine; I reverted to hiding it in a small handful of her favourite tasty mix, that very same mix which had been so abruptly denied her, one short week ago.

Now why didn't I think of that before?

CHAPTER 31

Being the reluctant recipient of a chronic illness myself, I have always believed that knowledge and understanding of any medical condition gives you a degree of control when trying to deal with the symptoms and I felt that this same axiom held true in Sadie's case. Having had no previous experience with horses other than the 'here's-one-I-made-earlier' lesson-ready riding school ones, I knew absolutely nothing about lameness or joint disease in horses. So, once again, I found myself scouring the internet for medical information – not for myself this time, but for my horse. In one sitting alone I found reams of advice and information on the different causes of lameness, from professionals and amateurs alike, coupled with an assortment of proposed methods of treatment ranging from the conventional to the unconventional and even to the downright whacky.

But I was willing to consider anything that had produced results in related cases. I tried using a magnetic device specifically designed for use on horses with osteoarthritis, together with various ointments and creams, in an effort to assist the healing process, but the days turned into weeks and still I saw no improvement. There were some days when I thought, yes, we're getting somewhere, and others when it seemed as if time had stood still and we were no further forward than we were on that very first day when I had brought Sadie in from the field. It was on those days that my spirits would sink and I would go home and weep with frustration at the injustice and futility of it all.

I discussed my options with Mike. I decided that if there was anything at all that could be done for Sadie I would do everything in my power to make sure that she had it. But I was reluctant to transport Sadie anywhere long distance for fear of exacerbating her lameness further, particularly when I thought back to her impromptu performance at the end of our previous visit to the medical centre.

After making more enquiries through the horsey grapevine, I finally heard about someone who was the equine equivalent of an orthopaedic consultant. Their practice was located in the next county, so travelling to our yard and back in one day, for a consultation, was feasible. The consultant vet came well recommended by other owners, but with a price tag (doesn't everything?). Mike was mindful of the costs but I suggested that there was no harm in making a telephone call to discuss Sadie's condition, and if nothing could be done for her, then at least it would put my mind at rest knowing that I had done everything I possibly could to make her better.

I made the call, knowing that I couldn't live with myself if I didn't. I found Vet very amenable and he gave me his full attention while I described Sadie's medical symptoms, the current treatment to date and my dilemma regarding further diagnostic tests versus any detriment a long road journey might have on her condition. After asking me a couple of questions, I knew my luck was in when Vet advised me that he had mobile equipment which enabled him to take X-rays and ultrasounds on site; he agreed to come to Kent to assess Sadie and I booked an appointment with him there and then.

A few days later he arrived for the assessment, pulling onto the yard in a fairly nondescript van that looked just like any other from the outside, but once opened became a veritable Aladdin's cave full of modern, high-tech equipment. I had never seen anything like it before; there was even a pharmaceutical dispensary in the rear section, full of every type of pill, potion and dressing that you could want. This was what I called impressive.

Vet gave Sadie the once over, asked me to walk her towards him, looked at her back leg and then turned to her front legs and remarked, 'I don't like the look of them either.' I was dumbstruck. He rolled up his sleeves, rolled out his gear, slapped one lead apron over his head, another over mine and set to work.

Sadie was sedated during the examination, as one kick to the equipment would render it useless and Vet was taking no chances – this kit was expensive! The X-ray machine was a modern-day marvel, programmed with a robotic voice that spoke to you, reading out the particular body part it was about to X-ray.

'Right hock blah, blah, blah,' then, 'Right front carpal blah, blah, blah,' chanted the monotone as it was put through its paces.

The pictures were then stored on a VDU screen under those headings, so that they could be easily found and reviewed by the vet immediately after he had finished. If the horse moved slightly or had an involuntary twitch just as the X-ray was being taken, the disembodied monotone would advise 'X-ray aborted', so you knew that it had to be set up again from that angle.

Following the X-rays, we moved on to the ultrasound. Vet shaved off Sadie's hair around the hock, smeared the area with a thick coating of glutinous jelly, and as the pictures came up on screen, he talked me through the findings. Every now and again there would be two or three other people from the yard, peering over my shoulder at the screen, listening intently to the vet's explanation, as curiosity got the better of them. It was like spending the afternoon on the set of *Casualty* and after several hours, Vet delivered his verdict. He confirmed that there was osteoarthritis in the right hock caused by the compression of the cartilage between the joints as well as a damaged ligament, but he went on to say that there was also extensive arthritis in the front legs and this degenerative joint disease was irreversible. He explained that this could be caused by repeated stress on the joints, such as jumping or dressage, and was quite common in competition horses.

Suddenly the penny dropped. This was why Sadie had been so reluctant to go over any small jumps or even poles on the ground. She was a well-schooled horse when she arrived and it was obvious that she had been a competition horse at one time in her life. But too much work had affected her legs, her joints would have been jarred every time she landed after a jump, so she had protected herself the only way she knew how and that was by rearing and refusing to jump. I also surmised that this was probably why her previous owners had decided to get rid of her. My poor baby!

However, all was not lost and Vet proposed a new medical regime. We would start Sadie on a course of injections, together with anti-inflammatories and a combination of supplements designed specifically for joint disease. I was also advised that it was worth looking at different types of leg supports for her, which work in the same way that compression stockings do on humans who spend long hours in bed. They would assist the blood flow when normal movement has to be restricted and would also help to prevent any swelling in the equivalent of Sadie's ankles. The difficulty would arise in managing her exercise routine, because although the damaged ligament required rest, box rest would aggravate the arthritis which needed light, controlled exercise.

We booked a follow-up appointment in four weeks' time to check on Sadie's progress, and as Vet doled out the necessary medications and supplements from his high-tech vetmobile, I tentatively asked about the bill.

'Don't worry about the bill, now. I'll pop one in the post to you in the next few days,' he said.

I expect this was a move that had been carefully calculated in advance, as no one wanted a delayed departure caused by shocked owners fainting at the size of their invoices.

When I arrived home, Mike asked how the assessment went and became very interested in the technical aspects of the mobile equipment whilst I extolled the virtues of modern medical science in the equine world. He then went on to ask a few cursory questions about Sadie's prognosis before his curiosity got the better of him and he could forestall the question no longer.

'Come on then – spill the beans,' he said. 'How much did he charge?'

'Oh, I don't know, honey,' I answered truthfully. Sounding as casual as I possibly could, I went on to say, 'Vet said he'd put the bill in the post to me.'

'Uh huh,' said Mike, and realising that any further enquiries regarding costs would be futile, he decamped to his office.

Vet was bang on the nose. His bill did arrive in the post a few days later, slipping silently through our letter box under cover of a couple of circulars and a gas bill. I tossed the envelope nonchalantly onto the kitchen table and waited for Mike to pop down to the shops. I watched discreetly as he pulled out of our driveway, and when he'd reached the point of no return, I rushed back to the table and ripped open the envelope with trepidation.

Did it cost an arm and a leg?

Yes.

Was it worth it?

In my opinion? Yes, yes, yes!

CHAPTER 32

Internet shopping was back on the agenda again – this time checking out equine medical supplies. Following Vet's recommendation, I surfed through a veritable cornucopia of equine leg supports, checking out the various makes along with the pros and cons of different designs. Having made my choice, I then discovered that I would need a set of bandages to keep them in place, or rather multiple sets, as I would need a clean set ready for use while the dirty ones were in the wash. Next-day delivery saw all my new purchases arrive safe and sound, and it was back to the yard for a crash course in bandaging. The staff at the riding school patiently showed me how to bandage the wraps around Sadie's lower legs without getting any creases or folds in the cloth, and as I watched the adept fingers swiftly wrap each leg, I thought how relatively simple my task was going to be. But, as with all things demonstrated by an expert, when it came to my turn, I soon discovered just how tricky the procedure was. The real expertise of bandaging lay in getting the tension just right – too tight and it would restrict the blood flow, too loose and the wraps would slip down the legs. Fearful of wrapping the bandages too tight, I often arrived at the yard in those early days to see Sadie in her stable looking like an aerobics teacher from a comic sketch, with her stretchy supports and baggy bandages all concertinaed down around the bottom of her ankles.

Every day I would take her supports off when she had her exercise, and an hour later I'd be bending down bandaging them back on again. The back ones were more labour intensive than the front ones because of their propensity for pooh stains, and when the weather was bad, the radiators of our bungalow became festooned with garlands of green bandages steaming silently as they lay draped along the tops to dry.

Another month flew by and, as arranged, Vet came back in his ubiquitous vetmobile. Despite Vet being based so far away, I found that the convenience of having Sadie examined at her own yard with the mobile kit far outweighed the other main disadvantage – that the vet was unable to attend at short notice. In addition, I found Vet very approachable and he was always available at the end of the phone if I had a query or needed to check some course of action.

We must have been doing something right because Sadie made good progress with her ligament, which was shown on the ultrasound as healing nicely, and her lameness, whilst still present, had improved. She was striding out more in walk, her trot was much better and overall she looked more comfortable. The pharmacy was raided yet again, with more injections, anti-inflammatories and supplements being handed out. A new plan of exercise was hatched. Vet suggested a programme to increase the controlled (!) walking gradually every couple of weeks, to get Sadie walking up to an hour a day and more, preferably split into two sessions, one in the morning and one in the afternoon. He then went on to include ascending ridden walk exercise over the next three months, if her condition continued to improve. I physically paled at the thought of some poor soul (probably me…) having to risk life and limb on a nutcase straight out of box rest and I put my fears to the vet.

'But, Vet,' I interjected, 'Sadie is her own worst enemy, it's her character, you see, those Arab genes from her dim and distant past that make her so excitable and difficult to handle. If there is nothing on the yard to spook at, she'll make something up and spook anyway, just for the hell of it. I'm concerned that as she gets fitter she'll become more difficult to handle, and I don't know how I'm going to manage to keep her at a controlled pace.'

Vet had the answer, as I hoped he would, and added a box of mild sedatives to the rest of the paraphernalia that was already laid out on the bench.

'Here you go,' he said, 'just give her a couple of these twenty minutes before her exercise and that should calm her down.'

CHAPTER 33

We were well into spring by this time and I had another pressing event vying for my attention besides Sadie… my wedding. Through all the mayhem, or maybe even because of it, who knows, Mike had suffered an aberration from his normally cool, calm and collected self. Despite the friendly warnings that such events needed to be planned a couple of years in advance, we had decided to press on with the arrangements for that year. We opted for a July wedding, in the hope that we might strike it lucky with a sunny day. But it was only when we set our plans in motion that we discovered what a mammoth undertaking this was going to be, and most of our free time was gobbled up with a multitude of tasks that seemed to materialise out of nowhere.

Where had the time gone? I don't know, but we were surrounded by things-to-do lists, schedules, checklists, itineraries, cost sheets and an array of other paperwork pertaining to the marriage, a large proportion of which was all laid out on our extended dining room table like a polemic strategy. I had no idea that arranging a wedding was so time-consuming and stressful.

We also tried to stick to a budget, which was a feat in itself as I soon discovered that the mere mention of the word 'wedding' seemed to double the price of most things. A small bouquet normally costing around £20 at the florists suddenly leapt to over £40 when the 'occasion' was mentioned and some rare cunning became essential if I was to achieve my goal. I am not ashamed to admit that I phoned all the wedding dress suppliers in our area to find out what sale stock they had and toured the retailers according to their responses. Without compromising on quality or design, I managed to buy a beautiful strapless dress in ivory silk for a fraction of its original price and did the same with my shoes, headdress and veil. There wasn't one item bought, or arrangement made, that we didn't haggle over or try to do a deal and most suppliers seemed to accept this. Whilst this may seem tedious to some people, it became a point of principle for us and I can honestly say that at the end of the day, we slashed our total costs by thousands.

Whilst we had both decided on having the actual wedding ceremony in our local village church, finding a suitable venue for the reception was another marathon task. We visited a vast range of hotels, country pubs, restaurants and manor houses during our search. This was a real eye-opener for me because everyone was quoting prices based on different things, and unless you asked the right person the right questions it was easy to assume a price included certain items when it didn't. Hotels, pubs and restaurants were easier to compare price-wise but the country and manor houses were a minefield. A quote would be given for the use of the property and grounds which in some cases included a marquee and in others didn't. Even worse, some places we considered did not have tables, chairs, linen, plates or cutlery in situ so these items were not included in their quotes. At these venues, the wedding couple were expected to hire all their dining furniture and tableware, napkins, chair covers, table cloths and literally everything else that was required, including the salt and pepper pots, and arrange for them to be delivered. Whilst there were specialist suppliers who looked after this aspect of the reception arrangements, it still involved sitting down with a price list and calculator, multiplying the individual cost per item (i.e. chair, napkin) by how many you *thought* you might need and then adding them all together. If numeracy wasn't your forte and you wanted to make a rough price comparison between venues, you needed nothing short of a mathematician to work out the final totals on your behalf.

We normally set aside our weekends to reconnoitre our shortlist of possible venues, and on those days I'd squeeze in a visit to Sadie either first thing in the morning or late afternoon.

As the search continued, we became quite adept at assessing the available amenities of each venue and we really thought we had experienced every variation and combination of additional costs that it was possible to budget for.

Until, that was, we turned up at one grand Edwardian country house of rather impressive proportions, set in lovely gardens. Having inspected the reception rooms, the dining room, the kitchen and the grounds, I enquired about the 'facilities' (being loo orientated myself by necessity, this was quite an important part of my agenda). I was shown a small cupboard-like room housing a tiny hand basin and a very old ball and chain flush WC and was told that this was the 'Ladies' Room'. Glancing over at my intended, who had a rather fixed look in his eyes that I'd seen before when boredom was about to set in, I then enquired where the Gentlemen were supposed to go. This seemed to rouse Mike from his reverie, and when the proprietor responded, 'We have a small outside WC in the garden for the gentlemen,' I knew we had his attention. Mike promptly decided that there was no time like the present to test the facilities and was quick to ask for directions. I ambled along in Mike's wake in a leisurely fashion, watched him disappear behind a trellis and played for time by engaging in some small talk with my hostess. When I heard the creak of rusty hinges from an old wooden door, I looked over my shoulder to see Mike emerging from the shadows, shaking his head slowly from side to side. I decided to probe further.

Expressing my concern that this would not be adequate arrangements for the eighty or so guests I was expecting, I asked, 'Are these the only two WCs available on the day?'

I stood in stunned silence as my hostess responded, 'Well, actually, we wouldn't expect all the ladies to be using the indoor WC anyway, because the loo is so old that the flush wouldn't be able to cope with all that use, so it is really only for emergency use.'

The plot thickens, I thought, as she continued.

'What usually happens is that the wedding party hire in a bank of Portaloos for the day and we have them assembled in the grounds.'

We then went on to have what I considered to be the most bizarre conversation about the different types of Portaloo that were available to hire, whether we wanted the 'standard' or 'de luxe' version and the corresponding cost of each. Somehow the image of my wedding guests drifting across the lawn, champagne glass in hand, to a bank of Portaloos, even if they were of the de luxe type, did not compare favourably with the picture

of sartorial elegance set in surroundings of timeless beauty that I had envis-
aged for my wedding.

As the car wheels scrunched on the gravel and we pulled out of the
grandiose gateway, I looked at Mike, found a pen in the glove compartment
and crossed yet another venue off of our list.

In the end, it was only by using our bargaining tactics that we were able
to book a venue for our reception which we would otherwise never have
been able to afford – a stately country house in the grounds of a wild animal park. Thrown in with the deal was the added attraction of being able to
offer our guests a safari through the park on custom-built trucks before we
sat down for our wedding meal. Safari versus Portaloos? No contest. Now
a safari was something really worth getting the hem of my dress dirty for.

When the invitations went out with the agenda for the day's events,
some of the guests were a bit bemused by the idea of a safari, but in the
end, most of them piled in, finery and all, and we all had a fantastic time;
although to be fair to Mike, I should own up to the fact that the 'rowdy'
truck was actually full of guests from my side of the family. Another plus
point of this venue was the added satisfaction of knowing that the profits
from our reception would be used for animal conservation and not for
lining the coffers of a corporate company.

There was also the question of where to go on honeymoon. You feel
almost pressured into going long haul because it's such a special holiday, but
somehow the thought of spending my first night with my new husband
shoehorned into an economy airline seat for hours, trying to get some
sleep, just did not appeal. I could have wallpapered the whole house with
the pages from the piles of travel brochures we amassed in our attempts to
find somewhere that we both fancied.

After much debate and dilemma we finally settled on a tour of the
scenic and unspoilt Azores, taking in some dolphin and whale watching
(which I was particularly keen to do) then continuing on to Madeira for
a week of relaxation before flying home. In all we planned to be away for
about three weeks and this was where my predicament over Sadie's ongoing medical care threatened to throw the proverbial 'spanner' in the works.

CHAPTER 34

Initially I was perfectly happy to leave Sadie in the care of the livery staff whilst I was away on honeymoon, as I had done for our previous holidays, but this time it was different. It was no longer a case of having her out in the field all day with the rest of the mares, just needing observation and a quick daily check to make sure she was fit and well. Now there was the issue of her medical care and controlled, but labour intensive, exercise regime by someone who was able to handle a horse that could be 'difficult' at the best of times. This was a responsibility that the livery yard was not so happy to undertake because of Sadie's unpredictable character, which meant that comparatively simple tasks were often likely to take longer than expected. She was my horse, and I only had the one to look after but staff on the yard had busy schedules, looking after lots of horses that all needed mucking out, exercising and daily care, and there are only so many hours in a working day. In extremis, I knew the yard would do their best, but Sadie really needed individual attention in a quiet environment, from someone who had the experience and time to monitor her progress.

Telephone directories were not the font of all knowledge they professed to be as I scoured the business sections for anywhere likely to be able to assist. My hopes were raised when someone, who had been in a similar situation to mine, recommended a small convalescent yard for horses that was little more than an hours' drive away. I telephoned the owners straight away, only for my hopes to be dashed when they told me they had given up the business recently because of other commitments. I tried various other ideas but none of them were suitable and, as my options dwindled, my nerves became more frazzled as time was running out.

Summer, or what passes for summer in England, was forging ahead and my initial unease over the situation gradually worsened until my concern escalated into nothing short of sheer panic as the days flew by. I didn't see how I could cancel the honeymoon without spoiling the wedding and setting off a family feud that would probably last for evermore, yet I knew I couldn't go away and enjoy myself when Sadie's health hung in the balance. I wasn't expecting miraculous results from her treatment. Vet had left me in no doubt that this was a degenerative condition and I accepted that I would probably return to find little or no change in her lameness. But I would find it very difficult to live with myself if, through bad management, Sadie suffered a setback, or worse, during my absence.

With one week to go before my wedding day and still no solution to Sadie's care arrangements, I sat with a few of the other livery girls at the yard, in a cloud of depression with my head in my hands.

'How's it going?' they asked.

'It isn't,' I responded, and we brainstormed a few more ideas between us until one girl said, 'What you need is a horse walker.'

'A horse walker?'

'Yes, one of those automated, circular pens that rotate at various speeds according to how much exercise your horse needs. You slot your horse into one of the sections so it can't shoot off anywhere; the speed is pre-set by the handler so the animal can only walk as fast as the machine rotates and bingo! All the work is done for you.'

'Fantastic idea,' I wailed. 'But I don't know anyone with a horse walker…'

'Paul has one,' she said matter-of-factly. Paul was her boyfriend who ran a small horse dealership on the other side of the valley and, although I had only met him once before, I knew he was well thought of on the horsey circuit.

'Paul has one?' I countered with surprise, a momentary note of brightness creeping into my voice.

'Yes, but Paul doesn't take liveries.'

'Aah…' I sighed, the seeds of optimism crushed before they were even out of the bag.

I stared at my dirty boots and my cloud of despondency threatened to settle once more when she mused, 'But I could ask him. He might consider taking Sadie in the short term, if I explained the situation. After all, it would only be for a limited amount of time, and of course, he'd be paid for his time.'

'Of course he'd be paid,' I reiterated.

'I could give him a buzz now if you like, see what he says.'

'Oh, please ask him if he will take Sadie for me,' I pleaded, not daring to get my hopes up. Paul would be perfect. He had spent all his life with horses and was so experienced. He would easily be able to handle Sadie, and I could trust him to make sure she was given her medication in her feed every day, consult with the vet or do anything else that was necessary. Yes, Paul would know exactly how to deal with Sadie and she could go in the horse walker every day for her exercise without shooting off at the drop of a leaf.

A phone call was made while I sat holding my breath and, to my utter relief, a tentative deal was struck. I could barely believe my luck, and we made arrangements to go to Paul's that same afternoon to check out the horse walker and discuss exactly what Sadie would need. I grabbed my cheque book and we all piled into his girlfriend's car, so that she could show me how to get to Paul's.

After a heart-stopping drive through the narrowest lanes I have ever driven down, we screeched to a halt in a cloud of dust, outside the gates of a small yard. Paul's place was clean and tidy with an outdoor arena, loads of grazing and stunning views across the rolling countryside. He ran it with his business partner, Ann, and most important of all they lived on site, so the horses were always under their watchful eyes.

Paul showed me the circular horse walker which was divided into quarters, enough to take four horses at a time if needed, and he expounded on its usefulness. Each section was big enough to take different sizes of horse, but was not large enough for it to turn around. A demonstration of this rather nifty contraption showed how the variable speed buttons could be set at slow walk, medium walk and boosted to trot or even canter if necessary. Sadie's stable wouldn't be five star, but she would be well looked after. I arranged for Sadie to begin with fifteen minutes of medium walk in the horse walker, both morning and afternoon, increasing this to twenty, then thirty minutes, according to how well she responded to the exercise. As Paul already had a free stable for Sadie to use, we decided that the sooner she was moved, the better; both for me (so I could now concentrate on the wedding) and for Sadie, so that her exercise regime could be implemented without further ado. I arranged a trailer for the following day and a cheque completed the transaction.

We then hurtled back through the countryside to the yard so that I could sort out all the kit that Sadie would need for her sojourn at Paul's. I bagged and labelled her medication and joint supplements, including a sheet of A4 paper listing how much and when she was supposed to have her various pills and potions.

The following morning I was a bag of nerves as Sadie's legs were wrapped in padded travel boots and a protective guard was popped around her tail for the journey. I decided to follow the trailer to Paul's in my own car, so that I could drive straight home after we had dropped her off. I couldn't trust myself not to burst into tears (or something silly like that) when the time came to say goodbye, and I could always beat a hasty retreat to my car if the floodgates threatened to open.

It was difficult to tell what was going through Sadie's mind when we arrived at Paul's, but she went straight into her stable and started to eat the hay he had placed there earlier.

'Well, that's a good sign,' Paul said. 'It hasn't put her off her food.'

No, that's true, I thought to myself, but then there's not a lot that *does* put Sadie off her food.

Then I met Ann for the first time. She had come out of the house to check on Sadie's arrival, and I was grateful for her constant chatter as she nattered away about all things horsey and local events. It didn't give me time to think, or become morose, about leaving Sadie.

I made a pact with Paul that I wouldn't visit Sadie again until after we had returned from honeymoon and that I wouldn't make any phone calls to check on her progress either. I gave him Mike's mobile number so that he could ring us in case of an emergency; I had made my decision to hand over responsibility for Sadie and now I had to let go and let Paul get on with the job.

With five days left to go before the wedding, I sat slumped on the settee that evening numbly watching TV, feeling like a dirty dishcloth that had been wrung out and hung out to dry.

CHAPTER 35

The day was perfect. Having been one of the wettest summers on record up to that point, even the weather decided to behave itself as the sun came out of hiding on the morning of the wedding. I had taken all my wedding clothes to my mum's house the previous day, and true to tradition, Mike had slept in our spare room while I tip-toed out of the house first thing in the morning, so that we wouldn't see each other that day before the church ceremony. A local hairdresser, who had been booked to put my hair up and fix my veil, arrived at my mum's mid-morning and set to work. My sister was there too, offering advice, helping me to dress and sorting out the finishing touches, like making some sandwiches for those with nervous stomachs and serving up copious amounts of tea. Shortly before the service was due to start she whisked Mum off to the church, where my brother was holding the fort as usher, together with Mike's best friend, leaving me and my dad to wait for the Rolls to arrive.

I had decided not to have any special make-up done for the day, as I wanted to feel more or less 'myself', but after much persuasion I did succumb to the purchase of a set of false eye lashes to augment my own sparse offerings. Following the instructions carefully, I had given them a practice run in the week before the big day, but they are quite flimsy items and I had struggled to clean the old glue off them without pulling them apart. Nevertheless, I thought I'd made an adequate job of it and afterwards I carefully stowed them away in their plastic box pending their public debut.

I didn't think I would be, but I was actually quite nervous on the day, and whilst I had applied my make up and 'falsies' with shaky hands, I was pleased with the result. I batted my eyelashes together a few times in front of the mirror to test out the enhanced effect and they seemed okay.

We were getting married at our local church: a lovely, quintessentially English village church dating from the 13th century, with an eye-catching oak-beamed ceiling and attractive stained-glass windows. Surrounded by adjoining farmland, the church is situated down a narrow track just outside the village, a short drive from my mum's house.

Bang on schedule, I heard a soft knock as the chauffeur rapped a gloved hand on the glass panel of my mum's front door.

I looked at my dad, 'He's here, then. Time to go.'

And my dad nodded back as he adjusted his waistcoat for one last trip up the aisle with his third and final offspring.

I had a quick look around, anxiously checking that I had everything I needed for the church and the reception, plucking my bouquet from its water pot at the last minute, wondering how many had been left behind, wilting in parents' and friends' houses, in those few final frantic moments before dashing off to the church.

Dad and I walked in silence to the car, lost in our own thoughts, and the chauffeur held the rear door open for me as I gently eased myself onto the soft leather of the back seat to avoid creasing my dress. I checked my strapless neckline (all safely gathered in there), but as I adjusted my veil to pull a diaphanous layer of flimsy gauze down over my face, something wasn't right – I had a blurred black line right in front of one of my eyes. I tried to focus on it to see what it was, but I couldn't quite make it out.

'Everything all right in the back?' said the chauffeur. 'Are you ready to go?'

'I'm not sure,' I mumbled. 'Hang on a minute. Where's my bag?'

I grabbed a small mirror from my handbag and whisked back my veil to find that one of my false eyelashes had come partially unstuck and was now teetering dangerously on the edge of my eyeball. I was mortified! It's that bloody glue, I thought to myself, what on earth am I going to do now?

'My eyelashes have come off,' I wailed and turned to my father, who stared back at me with a look of blank bewilderment on his face.

I could tell that there would be no helpful suggestions coming from that direction. Oh, what it is to be stuck in a Rolls Royce with two men totally unable to cope with such an emergency and not a woman in sight to assist with the crisis! I had no choice. I was too flustered to even think about refixing the thing and I couldn't go into the church with only one eye adorned with a set of falsies and the other one nude…

There was nothing else for it. I grabbed the dangling eyelashes from the corner of my eye where they hung like the sword of Damocles waiting to stab me if I blinked, peeled off the other set as well and shoved the pair of them unceremoniously into my purse, never to see the light of day again.

So much for the sales pitch of dark, luxurious lashes framing the eyes, I'd just have to put up with my own sparse specimens instead.

Needless to say that when we arrived at the church, Mike thought I looked beautiful and later said that he probably wouldn't have noticed any difference whether I was wearing false eyelashes or not. What was I saying about men…?

With the false eyelash debacle firmly behind us, our reception venue was everything and more of what I had hoped for our guests. Inside the mansion the hand-painted murals in the reception rooms were truly stunning, and from most viewpoints, courtesy of the weather, we were treated to magnificent views across the English Channel and beyond. The safari went off without a hitch, although there were some quips about people checking for missing body parts on their return… and the wedding breakfast was superb.

There were some disappointments, though. With the best will in the world, finances still dictated the length of the guest list and even some of those who were invited were thwarted by a massive traffic jam on the M25, which left them sitting in their finery in a queue of cars for more than five hours before they reluctantly called time on the event and had to make their way home again. On the plus side those coming from further afield had better luck and even cousin Stephen made it over from Australia in time for the wedding. As all the guests joked and chatted and supped champagne on the stately veranda, while the muted strains of classical music playing live in the mansion's grounds wafted over us, I sighed with contentment. Not a Portaloo in sight!

CHAPTER 36

The honeymoon was also a hit. Well, apart from an inter-island flight in the Azores which should have taken forty minutes and ended up subjecting us to a nine-hour tear-your-hair-out flight delay, but hey, the less said about that one, the better. Virtually untouched by tourism apart from the main island towns (and even there tourism is very low key), these islands are a stunning example of unspoilt natural beauty and fascinating geological phenomena. We visited three of the nine islands; Sao Miguel, Faial and Pico. Each of these islands has their own individual character, and we had such a lovely time that we have promised ourselves a return trip one day to visit the others.

Only a few days into our honeymoon, I spotted a leaflet in our hotel reception describing a two-hour ride on horseback through the Azorean forest. Unable to stop myself, I picked one up from the stand and started thumbing through it. Mike sidled up behind me and peered over my shoulder.

'I might have guessed… trust you to find a horse excursion,' he said in my ear.

'Have you seen this, Mike?' I said. 'It looks really good… they take beginners and apparently it's the only way to reach the totally unspoilt areas of forest. Here…' I said, thrusting the leaflet at him, '…you have a read.'

Having perused the contents, Mike was quite keen – on visiting the Azorean forest that is, as opposed to the horse riding aspect, but as that was the best way to see the forest, I managed to persuade him to take a look, at least, at the riding centre. Located just outside Ponta Delgada, on Sao Miguel, it was a short twenty-minute drive from our hotel, so we decided to call in there the next day.

The riding centre was run from a charming old ranch house built in traditional Azorean style with black pumice stone and whitewashed walls. As soon as we arrived I left Mike chatting to the owner, dealing with the business of how much for how long, whilst I rambled round the stable yard, checking out the horses and breathing in a cocktail of stable smells, like a drug addict one 'fix' short of cold turkey. I then wandered back to Mike to find he had 'taken the plunge' and booked us on a trek that afternoon. I was thrilled.

We returned after lunch and found we were to go out with another couple who were in a similar situation to us, in that the wife could ride and the husband was only a beginner. Our horses were sturdy, laid-back beasts and our guide was a very friendly Dutch girl who was on a working holiday during her summer break from college.

Under a warm Azorean sun we set off through a village of whitewashed houses, along narrow cobbled streets fronted by high stone walls. As we climbed higher, we soon left the village behind us and the narrow streets petered out into tracks where the vegetation grew gradually thicker until we were engulfed by the forest itself. The forest was dense and lush and dark and the horses picked their way along an almost invisible route through the undergrowth. All around us were a profusion of gigantic ginger lily plants, a towering and prolific species, not native to the Azores, that had unwittingly been imported to become the scourge of indigenous plants. The afternoon drifted by to the sounds of birdsong, the occasional snort of a horse and the rustle of vegetation as we brushed our way through the jungle-like terrain. It was magical!

Back at the ranch house I thought I saw Mike wince and rub his legs when he dismounted, so I mentioned that a good soak in the bath later on would probably help to ease any aching muscles that had been subjected to unaccustomed use. But in true man fashion, Mike nonchalantly declared that a few hours on horseback weren't going to get the better of someone like him – and if I detected a slight stiffness in Mike's gait the following day, I decided that the most tactful course of action was simply to ignore it.

However, of all the things worth mentioning, no trip to the Azores is complete without joining one of the licensed whale-watching trips that run from several of the islands, and the whale-watching trip that we took from the island of Faial was one of the highlights of our holiday. Whales inhabit deep water, and whilst there are no guarantees that you will see whales on any particular day, the ocean around the Azores plunges far deeper than the seas around Europe, which are restricted by the existence of the continental shelf. The warmth of the Gulf Stream flowing northwards coupled with the vast ocean depths make this area a popular haunt for both whales and dolphins, and sightings are common.

We had a choice between two different types of boat that were taking limited numbers of whale enthusiasts out into the Atlantic in search of these fascinating mammals. One was a rigid inflatable that had you strapped into your seats for the duration of the trip. Or there was a small cabin cruiser, a speedy little number that gave its occupants the chance to stretch their legs around a narrow deck, squeeze into a tiny cabin or climb up to a viewing platform on top of the cabin where the skipper and biologist, complete with binoculars for scanning the horizon, hung out. We chose the latter.

Now I'm not a salty old sea dog like my new hubby, who seems to have cast iron innards where sailing is concerned, but there again I'm not the worst sailor in town and we arrived at the harbour full of anticipation. We were barely ten minutes into our pre-departure briefing when the VHF crackled and our skipper received a message to say that a pod of whales had been sighted quite a distance out to sea and that we needed to get a move on if we were to catch up with them.

Our small group (Mike and I, another couple and a family) dashed down the gangway and, as soon as the biologist had cast off, our skipper gunned the motor into action and we were away. At full speed ahead it was a bumpy ride and no one warns you about the Atlantic swell. With no land mass for over a thousand miles in any direction from the Azores, there is nothing to stop the creation of powerful waves that give the boat a deep rolling, corkscrew motion, much like driving at speed round bends in the road, whilst cresting a continuous series of hump-backed bridges. My first mistake was moving into the cabin for some respite from the sea spray and my second was taking my eyes off the horizon to study the chart. As I sat inside the cabin with a fixed expression and clenched teeth, Mike was struck by my silence (an odd occurrence, I must admit…) and, glancing over, thought he detected a green tinge to my sallow complexion.

'You need to get outside on deck,' he said firmly, and despite my reluctance to move, he manhandled me out of the door and deposited me on one of the large buoys in the back corner of the boat, where I slowly regained my composure.

With the whales moving all the time it took us well over an hour at full throttle to catch up with them, and the long-awaited first shout of 'Whale ahead!' sent everyone scuttling to the deck railing for a better view.

First of all… nothing… then all of a sudden a fountain of water erupts into the air from the creature's blowhole and you spot the rest of the head floating on the surface of the ocean. But the most memorable sight of all is when the whale dives deep into the watery depths. As the whale's head gradually slips beneath the waves, you see the rise and fall of its arched back slowly follow, and just when you think the whale is about to disappear, you are rewarded with the awesome sight of its tail (or fluke as they call it) bursting from the sea and rising into the air like a banner. Then splosh – it's gone. Every time a whale's tail broke the surface and hung in the air for those few precious seconds, a gasp of delight rang out in unison from every single person on our boat.

The first whales we spotted were sperm whales, and then suddenly, the VHF crackled again and we sped off, further out into the Atlantic, in search of a pair of northern bottlenose whales which had been sighted by a lookout posted on another island. Apparently these whales are not such frequent visitors to that area and we were lucky to be graced by their presence.

We also saw a variety of sea birds that afternoon, and then a tiny sea turtle, swimming for all it was worth, on its way to a faraway destination. I was struck by the poignancy of this tiny creature, no bigger than the size of my palm, afloat on that great, vast ocean, so many miles from land. It appeared to be completely oblivious to our presence, fuelled as it was with its own dogged determination to return to its place of birth, with nothing to guide it but instinct, to lay its eggs and complete the cycle of life.

We had been at sea since lunchtime and by now it was late afternoon

– time to head back to Faial. I had claimed that buoy in the back of the boat as my own and with Mike's wet weather gear wrapped firmly around me I settled down for the ride home, sea spray 'n all. We made steady progress and, after a while, Faial appeared on the horizon.

Then a shout went up from the biologist, 'Dolphins ahead!'

Dolphins…? Despite feeling a bit worse for wear again, I wasn't about to miss out on the dolphins by being stuck at the back of the boat. The best views would be from the bow, at the front, but to get there I had to squeeze my way along a narrow piece of deck between the cabin and the boat's outer railings. Taking into account the rolling motion of the vessel and the fact that I was still minus my sea legs, I decided that the safest way to reach the bow was on my hands and knees. With one hand gripping the steel rail I crawled gingerly to the front, and the sight that met me took my breath away. There must have been at least fifty dolphins ducking and diving in front and to the side of the boat and all around the sea boiled like a cauldron with their bodies. Mike braced himself against the cabin behind me, trying to get some good shots with the camera whilst I lay prostrate on the deck, my head peering over the rail and my arm outstretched towards the dolphins as they took it in turns to 'surf' the bow wave, right next to our boat.

I was amazed at their speed and agility in the water. Our skipper was travelling at quite a rate of knots, or so it seemed to me, and sometimes I thought that the dolphins would come crashing into the boat in a head-on collision. But no, they were practised at the art, obviously having fun, and masters of the sea.

And then we saw it. It was the eagle-eyed biologist that spotted it first.

'Look,' she gasped. 'It's there. Right in front of us. Can you see it? The albino.'

My heart skipped a beat. An albino, a pure white albino dolphin!

These were Atlantic spotted dolphins, and this was the first time that our biologist had seen an albino dolphin in this area. I could barely contain myself.

I have always had a penchant for white animals. Why? I have often pondered that question myself. My white cat, with black splodges, that nobody wanted, my white horse, rejected and sent back to the dealer's, and now, right in front of me – a beautiful white dolphin!

What is it about their ghostly hue that strikes a chord within me and transcends the mundane? Is it because albino animals are sometimes shunned by their peers, resulting in a defencelessness and vulnerability that becomes a catalyst for my protective instinct? Is it that their whiteness gives them an aura of purity and innocence, so hard to find in today's world? Or could it just be the simplicity of their ethereal beauty that I find so compelling?

As I peered spellbound over the side of the boat, this white dolphin sped alongside us, wraithlike in the dark blue fathoms of water. And just as it had arrived, it disappeared, like a dream, and was gone.

CHAPTER 37

E ven though I had enjoyed every minute of our honeymoon, I was
looking forward to returning home, and now that the time had
come – I couldn't wait.

I promised Mike that the hectic pre-wedding agenda of 'things-to-do'
was now in the past; that on our return I would take things slowly and
ease myself gently into the flow of married life. I tried to be practical and
decided to spend the first day back organising the house, unpacking the
suitcases, sorting out the shopping, before I even thought about going to
see Sadie. But when I woke up that first morning, the suspense was too
much; I was bursting to see Sadie and the very idea of not seeing her until
the following day almost sent me into meltdown.

Mike wandered leisurely into the kitchen; I wondered how to broach
the subject.

'Mike, honey…'

'Yeeeh…'

'Oh, I'm dying to see Sadie… thought maybe I might go today after
all…'

'Today… when?'

'After breakfast…'

'After breakfast? I thought we were going to do the shopping this
morning. The fridge is empty, there's nothing for lunch or dinner, and we
haven't even unpacked yet,' Mike said.

'Aaw, honey. It doesn't really need both of us to do the shopping, does
it? Couldn't you go on your own while I pop down to see Sadie? – I won't
be very long,' I cajoled.

'Oh no, you don't. You're not getting away with that,' Mike said. 'You're the one who always complains that I don't buy the right stuff when I go shopping, and you're always quick to blame me if something gets forgotten. Anyway, you said you weren't going to see Sadie until tomorrow.'

Now what sort of a wife would I be if I didn't know how to win round my new husband? I turned on the charm.

'We'll have more time together later on in the afternoon. We can chill out and relax a bit, have a little lie down and… you know…' I said suggestively.

With my promise left hanging in the air, Mike relented.

'Oh, all right. I'll go to the supermarket and get all the shopping, but you'll have to help me write a list, so if anything's forgotten – it's your fault…' he paused, '…and I'll collect my brownie points later today…'

So we put together a list in double quick time, which was quite easy because the cupboards were bare. I chucked the first lot of dirty laundry in the washing machine, pressed the start button, donned my jodhpurs and shot straight out of the front door before Mike could change his mind.

I arrived at Paul's and no one was about, so I went round the corner to Sadie's stable, calling out, 'Sadie-bobs, I'm back!' (how silly is that…) and out pops her head over the stable door, ears pricked forward and still chewing a mouthful of hay. I rubbed her forelock, flung my arms around her and pressed my face into her neck.

'Hello, baby,' I murmured. 'Whatcha been doing?'

I brought her out of her stable and she seemed to be walking fine. Although her hock still looked slightly swollen, she seemed happy in herself.

It wasn't long before Paul was back – he'd taken one of his newly arrived horses out on a hack around the country lanes to get the measure of it.

'How do you know whether the new ones are safe to ride, Paul?' I asked, as he threw his leg over the saddle to dismount.

'I don't,' he said with a grin on his face. 'I just sling a saddle on their backs, jump on and say to myself: here we go again, let's see where we end up with this one, and then I take 'em out.'

Now that's confidence for you. In reality though, with Paul's experience, I suspected that he probably had a good idea about the horse before he got on it. On the other hand, I mused, there were no doubt a few little surprises that cropped up every now and again, even for Paul.

I asked him about Sadie.

'She's been no bother,' he said, 'and she's made friends with Ann's mare, the two of them are quite good buddies now.'

He went on to say that Sadie had got on well in the horse walker and that she was now doing half an hour's walk in the morning and half an hour in the evening without any ill effects. She was sound at walk (no longer limping) and was also doing well at trot.

I was so relieved to find that things were looking up.

As it was August and we still had a couple of months before the colder weather set in, I was eager for Sadie to spend more time out of her stable, in a more natural environment. In general, the consensus was the more time she spent out of her stable the less likely she was to run amok. Paul suggested sectioning off part of the paddock where Ann's mare was kept; we could make it big enough for Sadie to do a few paces of trot, but not big enough for anything faster, and the two mares would be company for each other. Paul was so practical. He had the electric fencing tape out that same afternoon and what became known as 'Sadie's Section' was soon in place.

At this point I decided that it would be a good idea to review her progress with the vet and when I arrived home that afternoon I gave him a ring. I explained that I had moved Sadie temporarily to another yard because it had a horse walker that gave me more control over her exercise programme, and we arranged an appointment for him to see her.

Over the next few weeks I got to know Paul and Ann. I was at their yard nearly every day, and I found their down-to-earth advice invaluable. Most days Ann was at the house when I arrived and she would always pop over for a chat while I was grooming Sadie.

Our little chats were always very interesting and I learnt a lot about horses; we didn't always talk about horses, but most things had a horsey connection.

Shortly after my return from honeymoon Ann was telling me about someone she knew who was going through a messy divorce (aren't they all?). This particular acquaintance had a couple of horses that she was now looking to sell because their house was on the market and she would have neither the land nor the money to keep them once it had been sold. Apparently her husband had absolutely no interest in anything equine and the inference was that the disparity in emotional attachment to horses between husband and wife had been a major factor in the breakdown of their marriage.

We talked generally for a bit about the devastation that divorce brings to everyone involved and how heartbreaking it is to part with animals that you have nurtured and loved. In pensive mood, Ann then went on to recall all the other couples she had known whose failed relationships were attributed to the fact that only one of them had a passion for horses.

'They never last, you know,' Ann said in conclusion, 'these marriages where only one partner is into horses. Horses are so time-consuming, they take over your life; there's always a conflict between the amount of time spent on the horse and time spent at home, not to mention the amount of money that needs to be spent on them.'

I pondered this fact as I picked up Sadie's tail and started to brush out the tangles. Hmm-ing, noncommittally.

There was another thoughtful pause in the conversation for a few seconds.

Then Ann said abruptly, 'Is your new husband into horses?'

'Well, no, not really,' I faltered, suddenly realising where the conversation might be heading.

Another pause.

'But he rides, doesn't he?' said Ann.

'Well, no, not really,' I said, fearing the death knell of the marriage about to toll.

'But I thought you said you'd been riding in the Azores.'

'Well, yes, we did, but that was more of a one-off, because we were on holiday, he's not really into having any regular lessons…'

'Hmm…'

Another pause.

'But I already had Sadie before he proposed, so he knew what he was letting himself in for before we got married,' I said defensively, hoping to redeem my situation.

Ann remained tight-lipped.

'And anyway,' I went on, not a little belligerently now, 'he's into sailing and I'm not, so while I'm out with the horse he's off on his boat.'

'Ah, well then,' Ann said, nodding her head sagely as if that levelled the playing field; we were obviously a well-matched pair of basket cases, both as nutty as each other and, therefore, in with a chance.

I breathed a sigh of relief. Phew, just sidestepped divorce by a hair's breadth.

CHAPTER 38

You know, it's funny how horses can always tell when they're dealing with a mug. I don't know how they know, they just do. Take Ann's mare, Poppy, for instance. She had such a timid, inoffensive nature that she needed a separate paddock because the other horses sensed her lack of assertion and bullied her.

It was this paddock that had been divided so that Sadie could have a small section of her own. Whenever I wanted to collect Sadie, I had to pass through Poppy's part of the field, which was also fenced with electrified tape. Whilst this was not a problem in itself, I had to switch off the battery-powered electricity supply, unhook the tape at one end and nip through the gap before securing the tape again. Most of the time Poppy was over on the far side of the paddock and ignored me completely when I walked through her part, so I became rather blasé about the whole manoeuvre.

One morning, I was just about to leave Paul's yard when Ann popped over and said that she had to go into town the following day for some shopping.

'What time were you thinking of coming tomorrow?' she asked.

'Around mid-morning, Ann,' I said.

'The thing is, Gillian, Paul won't be around in the morning either,' she added. 'He'll be away at a horse show and I won't be back until about lunchtime – will you be all right here on your own tomorrow?'

'Oh yes, I'll be fine,' I responded confidently. 'I know where everything is if I need anything.'

The next day when I arrived, I parked my car as normal, got my bits and pieces out of the boot and, whilst it felt a little strange walking onto the unusually silent yard, I wasn't at all concerned. I checked that the entrance gate was firmly closed behind me, picked up a headcollar and went to get Sadie in. As soon as I approached the paddock, Poppy's head shot up from ground level, where she'd been grazing quietly, and turned sharply towards me with her ears pricked forward like true north on a compass.

Hello, I thought to myself, what's up with her today? She doesn't normally pay me any attention. Better keep my eye on her.

I bent down to switch off the electricity connection and saw Poppy out of the corner of my eye, striding purposefully towards me. Puzzled by this uncharacteristic show of bravado, I hesitated for a few precious seconds, which was probably my undoing as it enabled Poppy to close the gap between her and the fencing tape. But I still had no idea that she was about to play me for a fool.

With one eye on Poppy, I unclipped the end of the tape to step through the gap into the paddock, and in the split second that the tape sagged to the ground, she kicked up her heels, shot into canter, jumped straight out of the field and careened off towards the yard.

I couldn't believe my eyes. I dropped the end of the tape like a red-hot poker and ran off after her with my heart pounding. She was normally so obedient with Paul, but that crafty old mare knew there was no one else on the yard and she was determined to make the most of her unfettered freedom. She led me on a merry dance: cantering around the barn, high-stepping away towards the arena, pausing momentarily for a hasty mouthful of forbidden fodder and teasing me with her unassailability. Her iron-clad hooves clattered here, there and everywhere while I tried to cut off her escape routes with outstretched arms.

After a fruitless five minutes or more I knew it was no good, she was too clever for me, dancing off with her tail in the air every time I got close. I needed to regroup and sort out a more tactical approach. I was also thinking about Ann and Paul – the only time I'm left on the yard on my own and I make a hash of it. How am I going to live this down? I had to get Poppy back into the paddock before Ann got home, so that no one would be any the wiser.

What to do? What to do? I thought frantically.

Then I had it!

I chucked a carrot in a bucket and wafted it around in front of her, while she eyed me warily. Then I opened her stable door wide, put the bucket in her stable and stood back. In she went like a dream, and I closed the door swiftly on her disappearing derrière.

While she was chomping on the carrot, I brought Sadie in and tied her up on the yard before taking Poppy back to the paddock and quickly resetting the electric tape.

I was just congratulating myself on having sorted the situation before anyone got wind of it, when a lady appeared by the entrance gate and called over to me, 'Do you need a hand?'

'Me?' I said. 'No. I'm fine, thanks.'

'Oh, I was just looking out of my window,' she said, 'when I saw Ann's mare running loose on the yard. Thought you might need a hand with her, that's all.'

Would you believe it? Ann's house was in the middle of nowhere and the only other place within viewing distance had the neighbour looking out of her window just as I was chasing round the yard like a headless chicken.

'Well, she did get out of the field, but I've popped her back now,' I said, trying to brush it off as nothing, 'umm, thanks very much for the offer.'

When Ann returned from her shopping trip I busied myself with Sadie, wondering how long it would take Ann to get to hear about my morning's fiasco, as the neighbour was bound to mention it at some point.

Sure enough, it wasn't long before Ann came over to me and said, 'Hear you had a spot of bother with my mare earlier on.'

My cover was blown, as I knew it would be, and I recounted my sorry tale, ending with, 'I think your Poppy was having a laugh, Ann.'

'Yes, I think she probably was,' Ann replied, and I swear I heard her chuckling to herself as she walked back to the house.

CHAPTER 39

With Vet's visiting day imminent, the burning question was how would he find his way to Paul's place along the labyrinth of lanes? There were hardly any road signs or street names to be seen, and those that did exist were often pointing in the wrong direction. Now I'm pretty useless at giving directions and I had visions of everyone driving around in circles for hours on end with no distinguishing landmarks other than fields of sheep to guide the way.

Picture this… Vet comes to a halt at a fork in the road and reaches for his mobile, 'Gillian, which lane do I take? Right or left?'

'Not sure, Vet, where exactly are you?'

'Not sure, Gillian, there's a field of sheep on my left and a dense hedgerow on my right…'

'Try the left turn, Vet, and you should come to an old barn after a mile or so, turn right…'

Half an hour later, I phone the vet again, 'Where are you now, Vet? Any sign of the barn?'

'No sign of the barn… but there's a field of sheep on my right and a rather familiar-looking hedgerow on my left…'

See what I mean? This wasn't going to get the job done or endear me to the vet, so I thought it prudent to rendezvous with him at our normal yard, so he could then follow me to Paul's.

On the appointed day, we met as arranged and set off in convoy to Paul's. Mindful of the value of the vetmobile and its precious cargo, I decided to go the long way round. This avoided the short cut down a narrow lane, where the overgrown brambles set your teeth on edge as they scrape the sides of the car, scoring deep and very expensive lines in the paintwork.

The first time we squeezed our way through this costly corridor, I had to ask whether it was an actual thoroughfare, although everyone in the know assured me that it was. Of course it's only the real locals that know about these obscure short cuts, so a relative newcomer like myself has little or no chance of finding their way and can easily become lost.

Anyway, we arrived without incident at Paul's and out came Sadie. I trotted her up and down a couple of times while Vet scrutinised her gait and Paul looked on with interest (why is it that no horsey person can resist the draw of a vet's diagnosis, especially when it's someone else's horse…). After some prodding of her bony joints, Vet declared himself satisfied with her progress and recommended that we continued increasing the exercise programme by adding short spells of ridden work to see how she fared. Although Sadie no longer needed the horse walker, Paul was happy for her to stay on at his yard in her dedicated section of paddock. It was still too soon to turn her out into a larger field with other horses, and I was grateful for his expertise.

Although I was eager to start riding again, I was apprehensive about the outcome because I knew that it would be the ultimate test for Sadie's joints. But I also knew that the sooner we started riding again, the sooner I would know if the long months of rest and rehabilitation had been a success.

I decided to 'go for it' and saddled Sadie up the next day for a walk in Paul's outdoor arena. We started off slowly and Sadie was on her best behaviour. It felt so good just to be riding her again, enjoying the gentle sway of her body as we took a leisurely stroll together. I chattered nonsense to her and stroked her neck with my fingers as we ambled along. In that moment I was at peace and it seemed as if everything in the world was in its rightful place. We only stayed in the arena for about fifteen minutes because I was determined to follow Vet's instructions and keep her ridden times short, gradually building them up if she remained sound. Everything seemed to be going so well until about two weeks later.

The approach road to Paul's was separated from Sadie's field by a motley collection of bushes that formed a tall hedgerow, and I soon discovered that by driving slowly along this road I could catch almost voyeuristic glimpses of Sadie grazing. Normally when I arrived at Paul's, Sadie was already in her 'section' in the paddock; but this time, as I slowed the car and squinted through the windscreen, there were no telltale flashes of white glinting through the gaps in the foliage – just clumps of green and patches of mud.

I felt a ripple of unease wash over me. I wondered if perhaps Paul was running late today and hadn't had the opportunity to put her out.

I pulled up and saw Paul on the yard with another horse. He looked at me as I walked through the gate and, without preamble, said, 'She's lame again, so I've left her in the stable for the time being.'

My heart sank and I asked Paul if anything had happened since the previous day that would have caused the setback.

'No,' he said. 'It's her hock again that's swollen and not only that, she's also lame on her front leg.'

I opened Sadie's stable door and ran my hand down her rear hind leg. Sure enough her hock was warm and swollen. In fact, there was virtually no difference in her poor swollen ligament since that first time I had brought her in from the field all those months before.

Despite all the hours of care, the weeks of box rest and the months of medication we were back to square one. I felt so frustrated and empty; I was totally out of my depth and I had no idea what to do next. Bereft of answers, I laid my head on her side and I wept.

Ann's head appeared over the stable door, and I hurriedly wiped the tears from my cheeks with the back of my hand.

'Not good news then,' she said matter-of-factly.

I was too close to tears again to risk a verbal response, so I shook my head slowly from side to side.

'You could turn her out, you know,' Ann continued. 'We had a mare once, damaged her hind ligament in a similar sort of way to your horse, so we turned her out for a year and, over time, it gradually healed itself. Nature is a wonderful healer. What are your alternatives?'

Ice gripped my heart as I considered what the other alternatives could be.

Sadie had spent the last six months on a mix of box rest and small amounts of limited exercise. Who was to say that she would be any better after another six months of the same, and anyway, that was no life for a horse. But it was Paul who put into words the dreadful reality of her relapse.

'You'll probably never ride her again, you know that, don't you?'

Never ride her again? Never sit on my Sadie-bobs and walk through the woods with her; never trot round the block with Nobelle and the other liveries; never go for a little canter across the fields together? I was heartbroken at the very thought of it.

'Not even if I turn her out for a year?'

Paul shrugged his shoulders. 'I don't know. Maybe. The ligament might heal itself over time but it's the arthritis in the joints, that's the other big problem. The best you can hope for is that medication will keep her arthritis at bay long enough for her to enjoy a spell of retirement in a field with her mates.'

He looked at me as my bottom lip trembled with the effort of keeping my tears at bay.

'You could always get another one,' he added brightly, 'plenty more horses about, all looking for good homes.'

I shook my head. I didn't want another one. I wanted Sadie.

Of course there was another alternative, the final alternative, which even Paul and Ann, as practical as they were, dared not voice in front of me.

CHAPTER 40

I told Mike the news as soon as I got home, and as he listened, I looked into his strong, blue eyes and remembered all the reasons why I loved this man. That was the effect he had on me; he gave me stability and restored some semblance of reason as I fought to control the emotional turmoil inside me. Oh, I admit, I found him infuriating sometimes, so measured and precise I wanted to ruffle him all up and watch him throw caution to the wind for just once in his life; but in reality, I probably did enough of that for the both of us.

Before we made a decision, I telephoned the vet and it was as we suspected. The arthritis was degenerative and Sadie would never be sound enough to be ridden again. But Vet agreed that retirement was a good option for her. He said he would pop by to reassess her in a couple of day's time and would leave me enough medication to deal with any inflammation and keep her pain-free.

Over those next couple of days I tried to stay positive, maybe Vet would come up with some other ideas or a different opinion, and I clung to the hope that there was a greater force in life that would see Sadie all right in the end. But when Vet arrived and ran his hands over Sadie's poor swollen joints, the look on his face doused that hope as he pursed his lips and nodded silently to himself. I knew what he was going to say before he said it, but the words still made me flinch.

'I'm afraid you'll never ride this mare again, there's too much damage to the joints,' he said. 'But I can keep her comfortable with medication if you want to retire her. She won't get better, but there's no reason why she shouldn't enjoy some quality of life if you want to put her out to grass.'

Mike and I discussed the options. Another spell of protracted box rest

156

was out of the question because that would only aggravate the arthritis. She had to keep her joints moving at a gentle pace but with a lot of rest in-between. She was young for retirement, most horses go well into their twenties, some even longer before they are retired, but there was no getting away from the fact that Sadie's joints were too damaged to take the weight of a rider, even a lightweight like me.

'What is it about owning Sadie that gives you so much pleasure?' Mike asked.

'How do you mean, honey?' I said.

'Well, is it the actual riding you enjoy the most or looking after her... or even the social aspect? I know you enjoy meeting up with all the girls on the yard... or is it something else, something deeper?'

'Oh, it's something much, much more than just the riding,' was my immediate response, and I tried to explain. 'Whatever happens during the day, however stressful or tedious or just plain boring my day has been, as soon as I see Sadie it's all forgotten. I get pleasure from just simple things, like watching her, cuddling her, feeling her warm breath on my hands as she nuzzles me for titbits...'

'I know her inside out and love her dearly. I admire her quirky, headstrong nature and her courage; despite everything she's been through, and her failing health, she still fights for life. I can see my own health problems reflected in hers, the various flaws that both of us have had to learn to live with. I look at her and think, if she can fight back through her pain, then so can I, and when I see her rise up against the odds, she lifts my spirits too... it makes me feel that I can also rise above my problems.'

'Then there are our quiet times together that I enjoy so much. I love spending time with her, grooming her, going all over her body with regular, even brush strokes, watching her head relax and her eyes close, emptying my mind of everything except those long, rhythmical strokes and her soft, warm body.'

'...And there's the added benefits I've gained from regular exercise, mucking out her stable, being out in the fresh air...' I said, trying to think of the more practical side of owning a horse. But although I struggled to explain what Sadie really meant to me, I couldn't find the right words.

I felt that there was something more, some fire that she quenched, something indefinable so deeply entrenched within me that I was unable to express it in words.

But it was enough for Mike. He put his arm around me.

'You can still ride any one of the riding school horses, can't you?'

'Well, yes… I can,' I replied.

'And you'll still have your own Sadie, to fuss over and spoil, won't you?'

I nodded into my wet tissue.

'Well then, retire her. Bring her back from Paul's, turn her out in the field with the other horses and think how happy she will be with a nice mum like you to look after her…'

CHAPTER 41

Once I had taken the decision to retire Sadie, I felt much happier within myself. I knew it was the right thing to do, and I made arrangements to have her transported back to the yard, to her own stable, her old friends and familiar surroundings; back to the big field that she shared with the other horses, where she could live in peace with no one making demands on her fragile joints. With such a large field and access to gentle grazing round the clock, Sadie wouldn't have any pent-up energy that was commonly caused by box rest and she would also live as close as was possible to a natural life for a horse.

Vet had also discussed with us the option of removing her shoes if we were going to retire her; she would have a better grip in the field without them and having her shod every six weeks was an unnecessary expense when she was no longer being ridden.

I spent my last morning at Paul's collecting Sadie's stuff and tidying up. It would be good to get Sadie home again, but I had enjoyed the weeks with Paul and Ann, and quite frankly, I don't know what I would have done if they hadn't stepped in at the last minute to take Sadie. While I was waiting for the horsebox to arrive, I tied Sadie up on the forecourt and flicked a brush over her for want of something to do.

Ann was pottering about and sidled up to me. 'Have you given any more thought to what Paul said? About getting another one?'

'No, Ann,' I said, 'Sadie is all that I ever wanted in a horse.'

'I'm sure she is,' she said in her direct manner, 'but if you'd bought this mare as a youngster, with no health problems, you do realise that someone with your limited experience wouldn't have been able ride her. So often when people come to us looking for a horse, they have a mental image of the type of horse that they want to buy – sometimes it's an idealistic one… of a fine-boned thoroughbred type of horse. But they don't realise that along with fine breeding comes an excitable and sometimes nervous temperament that only an experienced rider can handle. What most people should be buying is a sturdy cross-breed; a horse that will hack out across the countryside without bolting off, that won't get bored in an arena practising routine exercises with a novice rider. If we think that a horse isn't suitable for someone, we try to tell them, but some people won't listen.

'So, think about it,' she continued, 'not what you want, but what you need.'

Ann paused to let her words sink in.

'We can always keep an eye out for you, if you like, because it might take a long time for the right horse to turn up,' she added.

'I know you're probably right, Ann, but I'm not thinking about anything at the moment,' I said, 'just Sadie.'

Ann shrugged in resignation as the horsebox pulled up outside the gate and started reversing onto the drive.

'Well, you know where to find us, don't you? Just give us ring.'

Sadie's transfer back to our yard went without a hitch, and I popped her into a stable for the first night so that she could reorientate herself to her old surroundings. The farrier was due at the yard in a couple of days and I had arranged to have her shoes removed during his next visit.

I wanted to turn her out into the big field with the other mares as soon as possible, to see how she would cope. But I was apprehensive. There were a couple of new horses in the field that didn't know Sadie, and with the dynamics of the herd now changed, I wondered if she would be accepted again. In addition, she was more vulnerable now that her mobility was impaired and I was concerned for her safety.

When I arrived at the yard the following morning I came well prepared. I had decided to keep a watching brief on Sadie while she was reintroduced to the herd, just in case there was trouble, and to keep me occupied during my vigil I had brought a flask of hot tea and a magazine.

We took a slow walk along the lane, but Sadie knew exactly where she was going and her ears went forward in anticipation. There were no horses nearby when we reached the gate, just a small group grazing together about halfway across the field. I closed the gate quietly behind us and slowly took off Sadie's headcollar.

'Go on, girl, off you go,' I whispered, patting her neck as I released her.

I moved to one side, stashing my flask out of harm's way behind a fence post, and watched Sadie take a few steps towards the others, before coming to a halt, her attention fixed intently on the grazing group. Then I noticed a stocky black cob jerk its head into the air, to stare back at the newcomer for a second or two. Suddenly it broke away from the others, leapt into canter and headed straight for Sadie. Sadie just stood there waiting… motionless… and I held my breath, transfixed, not knowing what to expect. Surprised by this swift spurt of energy from one of their own, the rest of the herd decided to follow at a more leisurely pace, to see what all the fuss was about.

For one heart-stopping moment I feared the worst, and it was only as the black cob skidded to a halt in front of Sadie that I recognised her. Cleo stretched out her neck as Sadie lifted her head and they touched each other tenderly on the nose, a gesture of old playmates unexpectedly coming together again after a long and lonely absence. Something seemed to pass between these two mares as they touched, something transient but nonetheless real, something that they both understood, because Sadie relaxed her head to the ground and started to graze, oblivious to anything else, while Cleo danced joyfully around her, warding off any other horse that deigned to get too close to her special friend.

My job was done. I collected my flask and my magazine from behind the fence post; there was no need for me to stay any longer. With a guardian angel like Cleo looking after her, Sadie had nothing to fear from the other horses; Cleo was a formidable foe and an even greater ally.

I had set my horse free in the best way I knew how: in a large field with her friends, to enjoy her retirement.

CHAPTER 42

In addition to the upset that Sadie's early retirement had caused, something else had been nagging at me, doggedly, since our return from honeymoon.

Perhaps it was an innate response to our recent wedding that triggered some kind of 'nesting syndrome' in me, but I had been struck with an overwhelming urge to renovate the only room left in our bungalow that hadn't been revamped since we bought it.

We had been putting 'our stamp' on the bungalow ever since we had moved in. Starting from the top and working our way down, the first requirement had been a new roof. Mind you, as the old one started leaking shortly after our arrival, that expense was a bit of a necessity. One evening I was sitting in the lounge when I happened to glance upwards to see the Artexed ceiling of our lounge start to sag without warning, distending heavily downwards like a cow's udder ripe for milking. Before my brain had even registered the possibility of impending doom, the textured udder ruptured in front of my eyes and deposited a stream of brackish water onto the carpet without a by your leave. Over the next few weeks more sodden patches appeared on the carpet until it was chequered with a colourful assortment of buckets and bowls; the new 'must-have' accessories, as I explained to friends and family when they popped round for a visit. Claims were made, disputes settled and nine months later we had a new roof.

Next was the en suite for our bedroom. Now that was another essential, because we only had one bathroom in the house and Mike was fed up with being ousted out of it at a moment's notice whenever my colitis dictated that I needed immediate access to the loo. With the en suite taking a chunk out of our savings, Mike decided he should be compensated with a new wet room in place of the old family bathroom, which had a rather passé blue suite that neither of us liked anyway.

Then there was the new bedroom furniture... because it was half-price in the sale with further reductions, and I didn't have enough wardrobe space – is there a woman on this earth who does? And that just left the kitchen...

Now, I felt, it was time for the kitchen to be 'seen to'. Mike was opposed to all the upheaval that this would entail and I wasn't exactly looking forward to it myself, but help came from the most unlikely source when my niece found herself a new job with a kitchen supply company.

'If you want a new kitchen, Auntie, we get a good staff discount on all kitchen units as well as appliances,' she said.

She had my immediate attention. So later that week, on her way home after work, my niece brought round one of their catalogues together with a copy of the coveted trade price list and I sat down to earmark my favourites from the different ranges.

Picking my moment, I cuddled up to Mike on the settee as we sat watching the TV and whipped out the brochure.

'What's that you've got there then?' he asked distractedly.

'The latest kitchen brochure, babe,' I said and proceeded to sigh longingly over my favourites. 'Ooh, look at that one, Mike, isn't it lovely...?' I cooed.

Despite his objections, his interest was piqued, and when the TV adverts broke his concentration, I stepped into the void.

'What an opportunity! It's too good to miss...' I pressed. 'Look at these prices... and we get a further "staff" discount as well... you know how expensive kitchens are.'

Fortunately, Mike agreed with me.

Having made our decision to go ahead with a new kitchen, we were thrown into a frenzy of plans, measurements, styles of units, appliances, worktops and wall tiles – not to mention the flooring, fitters and plumbers. As we became further enmeshed in the details of the new kitchen, I have to admit that I totally underestimated the amount of work that it would entail.

Suddenly even the simplest of things took on epic proportions: decisions about power points, how many and where should we put them, which type of corner unit to go for, should we have drawers and where to put the cutlery holder and the wine rack, to name but a few. Then there were the taps; who would have thought that there were so many different styles of the humble kitchen tap? Get it wrong and the whole kitchen was destined for failure... if anyone had ever said to me that I would lose sleep over a kitchen tap, I would never have believed them. Perhaps that's the trouble with this world of ours, too much choice.

Lighting was another issue that was crucial to the success of our kitchen. I was determined to get spotlights that actually illuminated the sink and worktops without my big head casting a shadow over everything while I was trying to cook. So we decided to call in our electrician and have the new lighting all wired into the ceiling before the kitchen fitters set to work. This was when we discovered that, under the grease-stained Artex, our kitchen ceiling was actually old lathe and plaster, which fell away in great chunks when the electrician cut the holes for the new sockets.

'Ceiling will have to come down,' he informed us. 'That old lathe and plaster needs either boarding over or replacing.'

'Yikes!' I said. 'Can't you just patch it up with a quick skim?'

'Nope, can't do that either. Any extra weight on that ceiling will bring the whole lot down.'

Great! Another 'little job' we hadn't bargained for.

Before we could get on with anything else, our next task was the removal of all the old kitchen cupboards, barring the sink unit, which was to be left intact until its removal was deemed an absolute necessity. DIY was definitely not Mike's forte but he did make a reasonable demolition man, and he spent several days reducing the cupboards to their original, embryonic 'flat-pack' status, while I shoved the resulting debris into the back of my estate car and drove it round to our local recycling depot. A week later we surveyed our handiwork. Our kitchen had been reduced to a bare, grey concrete shell with exposed wires dangling through gaping holes in the ceiling and only a solitary sink unit, covered in lumps of plaster, remaining... not unlike those bombed-out buildings that journalists are so fond of standing in front of as they deliver their latest updates via satellite link from a war zone.

But worse was yet to come. During the entire process, we seemed to lurch from one crisis to another, and Mike's fears about my ability to cope with the whole undertaking came to fruition when the sink was finally disconnected.

In our efforts to retain some semblance of domestic normality, we had set up a kitchenette area on an old desk in the lounge where we stashed the kettle, tea bags, coffee, sugar and soft drinks together with a motley array of mugs, plates, pots and pans, as the rest of the kitchen paraphernalia had been packed away in boxes. This was not only for our own benefit but for the workmen too, who always seemed to do a better job if you plied them with tea and coffee during the day; not to mention the can of Red Bull, that did wonders for the chap who came late one afternoon to top up the loft insulation when the wiring was finished.

All of this inconvenience was just about manageable, until we lost the kitchen sink. Sadly it seemed that out with the sink went my sanity. Up to this point the kitchen sink had enabled me to carry on with the cooking, albeit producing fairly modest meals; without the sink, however, I was now unable to do any washing up. The pots wouldn't fit in to the bathroom sink, and I had nowhere to drain them afterwards.

When Mike suggested they all go in my bath I was thrown into a fit of apoplexy, declaring, 'No way! Don't even think about it! Under no circumstances, not even ones as dire as these, are any of those greasy pots and pans going into my new bath!'

I had splashed out on one of those new-fangled air-baths that shot warm air through pinholes in the bottom to create a Jacuzzi effect, and I could just imagine it – lying back in the water, scented candles setting the scene, turning on the bubbles in expectation of fragrant aromatherapy oils and what do I get?… globules of cooking grease trapped by those tiny holes, floating to the surface. Not on your life!

I have never been an avid fan of takeaway meals but friends and relatives all pronounced that it was the only solution to our dilemma. Maybe I was being too harsh on these high street hubs of cooking activity.

Perhaps it was about time I dragged myself into the 21st century and forgot about peeling spuds and making my own cheese sauces. So following the demise of our kitchen sink, I relented and Mike was despatched to the nearest establishment to pick up our evening meal. On his return, it was quite exciting, unwrapping those little parcels of food to see what each one contained and eating from greaseproof paper like kids on a camping holiday. I actually quite enjoyed my dinner, but alas, I was unused to fatty, fried fritters and foreign fare and, as the evening progressed, the meal lay in my stomach like a lump of lard until it transited my poor debilitated digestive system quicker than a bat out of hell.

As always, it was my mum who finally came to the rescue. Oh, the relief of it when she said, 'Just bring it all round here, dear. You can't carry on without a proper meal inside you.'

I ended up taking most of our food round to my mum's, where we would stand at her kitchen sink chatting and preparing vegetables, like we used to do when I was still living at home. In fact, Mike is convinced that I haven't really left my mum's at all, according to him I'm always rushing off round there despite being married.

Anyway, I would load the ready meal into the car, serve it up at home and then pile all the dirty dishes into various receptacles to be stashed overnight pending their despatch to Mum's dishwasher the following morning.

The knock-on effect of having no sink meant that there was also no connection to the washing machine, and it wasn't long before the dirty dishes in the back of my car were accompanied by an assortment of dirty washing, all destined for my mum's house too.

Throughout everything it was my Sadie who kept me sane. She was my refuge in times of stress, and I would shut the front door with a surge of relief as I left the house to see her. I would bring her in from the field and spend an hour or two on the yard with her, brushing her down, checking her winter rugs and seeing to her medication. But despite plying her with an assortment of Vet's pills and potions, that uncompromising arthritis roamed her body like a voracious gypsy, seeking out pastures new as it moved indiscriminately from joint to joint. Sometimes she was lame on her front leg, sometimes on her back leg, sometimes I thought I couldn't detect any lameness at all and at others… my heart went out to her as she hobbled along behind me.

Occasionally, I booked a ride on one of the school horses, but whatever free time I had, Sadie always took priority. She was my port in a storm; there was no rushing around when dealing with Sadie, no last-minute panic. Not like the day when the kitchen tiler arrived.

In my experience, good kitchen tilers are hard to find and even harder to book because they are usually so busy. When we started dismantling the kitchen back in October, I was ignorantly confident that by the end of November we'd be all done and dusted. Oh no… not even in my dreams! It is not just the fitting of the kitchen, but arranging all the different workmen to arrive in the proper sequence that takes the time. Most of the workmen seem to have a different agenda and, in general, all of them have a number of jobs on the go at once. Then, even when the kitchen is eventually all fitted and plumbed in, you need at least a fortnight for the decorator to come round and finish off all the gaps and rough edges before he can put the final coat of paint on the ceiling and walls. Now, we were looking at a finishing date of just before Christmas, and if I was to make the Christmas deadline, everything needed to run like clockwork for the last four weeks.

Not only did we need someone to do the wall tiling but our new utility room also needed floor tiles to be laid.

Our kitchen fitter had shown the tiler the kitchen plan, detailing which areas were designated for tiling, and he had declared, 'I can just about squeeze that job into a day's work. I'm on another job, you see, and if it's just one day then I can fit it in around the plasterer at the other place. But I'll have to get started early and it probably means I'll finish late. Otherwise I won't be free for about another three weeks.'

Three weeks! I gulped.

'No problem at all,' I said in dulcet tones. 'You can start whatever time you like, we'll have everything ready for you.'

'Crikey!' I confided to Mike. 'Our tiler's going to have to go some to get that lot done in a day. What do you think?'

Mike raised his eyebrows. 'Well, he knows his job, so he should know how long it will take him. What time's he coming in the morning?'

'Seven thirty,' I said glumly, already feeling sleep deprived. 'That'll be another crack of dawn wake-up time for me, if I'm to get in and out of the bathroom, have my breakfast and go to the loo before the workmen arrive.'

We got all the boxes of tiles in from the garage the night before and stacked them in the kitchen. There were three different colours for the small wall tiles, shades of terracotta and cream, to be mixed randomly and set between the worktop and the wall units, and we put them in their respective piles. Perfect!

True to his word, the tiler arrived at seven thirty the next morning and set up his tile cutter and other gear. I showed him the boxes of tiles and he was off. By eight o'clock he had completed the first row on a small section of wall and was just starting the row underneath when he said, 'Did you know that these tiles are slightly "off"?'

'Off?' I queried at a loss. 'What do you mean by "off"?'

'This beige-coloured tile here…' he said, tapping the tile with a metal scraper, '…is fractionally larger than the other two sets of coloured tiles.'

He put all three colours side by side and you could barely distinguish any difference between them at all, but when you put them on top of each other, you could see that one of the coloured tiles was marginally larger than the other two colours.

'What does that mean?' I gasped.

'Well, I might get away with it on a small area, but the more we build up the rows of tiles, the more out of alignment they'll become.'

'Oh my God! I can't live with that. Every day looking at my kitchen tiles not lining up properly will drive me potty.'

'Mike!' I screamed, reminiscent of a NASA space launch, 'we have a problem!'

Closer inspection revealed that the batch numbers were different on that particular set of tiles.

'There's nothing else for it. They'll have to go back,' I said.

Mike tried phoning the warehouse.

'No reply,' he said. 'They're probably not open yet, we'll have to wait.'

The tiler looked at his watch.

'I've only got today to do this job, love,' he said to me.

Panic stricken, I grabbed Mike in the hallway and said brusquely, 'Take the tiles and go back to the shop.'

'But they're not open yet!' he hissed back at me.

'Never mind. They might have opened by the time you get there. Bang on the door if necessary, there's bound to be somebody about, they deal with builders, for goodness' sake,' I said in desperation.

'But we don't even know if they have the right batch number for this colour,' Mike continued, all calm and logical.

'Then get another colour. We'll lose the tiler if we can't get those tiles exchanged this morning, and then we won't be finished by Christmas,' I said through gritted teeth as I shoved Mike out of the door.

I turned to the tiler. 'Perhaps you could start on the floor tiles in the utility room?'

'Not really, love, can't do the floor until I've done the walls,' he said matter-of-factly.

'My husband won't be long,' I said, feigning calm. 'I'll put the kettle on.'

Unable to stand the suspense, I left the tiler sorting through the floor tiles in the utility room, ready for cutting, and decamped to our bedroom to have my nervous breakdown.

Mike's frantic early morning dash across town paid off. Just as he arrived at the warehouse, the chaps were pulling up the shutters. Luckily they did have the right batch number for that colour tile, and Mike had the correct tiles in the car before you could say Jack Robinson.

I grabbed the phone as soon as it rang.

'I've got them. I'm on my way home. Tell the tiler I'll be there in about fifteen minutes.'

My pulse didn't return to normal until Mike walked through the door with the new batch and the tiler nodded in agreement that these were, indeed, the right ones.

Phew! I was exhausted and it was only 8.45 in the morning.

But, give that man his due; our tiler worked like a Trojan, straight through the day with only a short break for lunch. By seven o'clock in the evening I was sitting in the lounge pretending to watch TV, tapping my feet with barely disguised impatience, when I finally heard the magic words, 'All finished, love. I'll just pack the van up and then I'll be off.'

I dashed into the kitchen for a quick assessment before the tiler disappeared into the night, never to be seen again. But despite the fraught beginnings, I needn't have worried. He'd done a lovely job and we were both really pleased with the result.

The front door had barely closed before I ran back into the kitchen, grabbed the frying pan and slung in some eggs for a quick omelette before Mike and I both fainted from hunger.

CHAPTER 43

I t was touch and go, but the kitchen was just about finished in time for Christmas. I waved goodbye to the last of the workmen with a sigh of relief on the day before Christmas Eve.

Christmas presents had been replaced this year with gift vouchers, our artificial Christmas tree remained firmly in its box in the loft, but I didn't care. We had the best Christmas present ever – our new kitchen.

The modern units all shut silently on their soft-close hinges and all my appliances were plumbed in and operational. Our old wooden kitchen table had been replaced by a more modern counterpart, the floorboards were no longer strewn with workmen's tools, I could finally reach my new sink without having to step over a plumber's backside, and the cat had decided it was now safe to enter the house during daylight hours.

Gone were the days of piling dirty dishes, pots and pans into every available container and carting them off to my mum's; all the crockery was at my fingertips and I could open my cupboard doors at will to find them all neatly stacked alongside the groceries. Even those small innocuous items that you never take any notice of until you can't find them, like a pair of scissors or a ballpoint pen that actually worked, were now back in their rightful places.

After what seemed like months of living on a building site, all that remained was the big clean-up. The sawing and drilling had taken their toll on the whole bungalow, and there wasn't a shelf or table top that hadn't been assaulted by a fine layer of dust.

On Christmas Eve I was up early. First of all I shoved a bottle of champagne into the fridge (got to get your priorities right…), then I donned my plastic gloves and set to work. I concentrated on the kitchen, the dining room and the lounge, Mike chipped in to hoover the carpets and at the end of the day we celebrated our efforts by popping the cork on the bubbly and putting our feet up.

Now that we were the proud owners of a brand new, fully functional kitchen we decided that we should celebrate our return to normality by having a Kitchen Party. Most of the family were otherwise engaged over the Christmas week, so we decided to invite everyone over for lunch on the first weekend after New Year, when most people were winding down in expectation of their return to work. This was quite a leap of faith for me as I am not a 'party' person and am relatively inexperienced at organising any sort of social extravaganza. However, I deemed that on this occasion a special effort was merited and I was looking forward to having the family round.

After much deliberation over the best way to tackle this unexpected challenge, I decided to keep things simple by opting for a lunchtime buffet where people could help themselves. I took charge of all the food and delegated responsibility for the selection and serving of drinks to Mike; a task to which he applied himself with some relish, I might add.

I did most of the shopping and food preparation on the Friday and then popped up to the yard to check on Sadie in the afternoon. I brushed her down, checked her feet, gave her a cuddle and some carrots and put her rugs back on. It was going to be another cold night but I knew Sadie would be all right – she was wearing two thick coats and was buckled up to the throat in a cosy neck cover.

'Won't be in tomorrow,' I called out to the girls, as I was leaving the yard. 'See you all on Sunday.'

By Saturday morning the house was spick and span and my best embroidered table cloth had been laid out with a flourish on the dining room table. I spent the morning setting out dishes of cold meats, smoked salmon, salad and dips in the dining room, and while Mike was setting the scene with some 'chill-out' music, I changed my clothes and slapped on some make-up. Most of my family live locally so they were all expected to arrive around midday. It was pushing twelve already and I was just putting some half-baked bread rolls into the oven to finish cooking, when the phone rang.

'Can you get that please, Mike; I'm just opening the oven door,' I called out, thinking it was probably someone running a bit a late.

Mike's frame appeared in the doorway. He looked at me and held out the phone.

'It's for you,' he said. 'It's the riding school.'

'The riding school?' I said, perplexed.

I threw off my oven gloves and took the handset.

'Hello?'

It was the owner of the yard.

'Gillian. It's Sadie. She's lying down in the field. We haven't seen her move at all so I'm sending someone up to check on her.'

'But… but she often lies down in the field. I-I'm sure she's all right…' I stammered.

There was an awkward moment of silence at the other end of the phone that I found unnerving, and I continued, 'I'm just expecting some of my family over for a lunchtime party; do you think I should come to the yard, I could probably get away in a couple of hours?'

'No, don't do anything yet, let's wait until Sara gets back from the field first.'

'Please phone me as soon as she does,' I said anxiously.

'We will. Bye.'

I listened for a few seconds to the dull hum on the line as the connection went dead, and a feeling of deep unease crept over me.

'I have seen her lying down in the field before,' I said by way of explanation to Mike, but my words sounded hollow as I recalled the note of concern in the voice of the caller.

'What do you think I should do, Mike? Should I go to the yard now?' I asked, when I told him what had happened.

'I don't think you should do anything at the moment,' he said. 'As you say, you've seen her lying down before – there's probably nothing wrong, but if there is, the yard will know exactly what to do, whatever the circumstances. They'll know how to deal with Sadie, and if they need to call a vet, you can pop over there after lunch. Anyway, we don't know anything for certain, yet.'

'Yes, I expect you're right,' I said, brushing my concerns to one side. 'It's probably nothing serious.'

Just then the doorbell went. It was my dad first of all. Then my sister and my mum and some of my nieces, all arrived in quick succession and were duly shown into our new kitchen, for the guided tour. Everyone responded appropriately with the right number of oohs! and aahs! as integrated appliances were revealed, worktops were caressed and doors and drawers were opened and shut on the soft-close hinges that operated to perfection.

It wasn't long before everyone gravitated towards the food, so I whipped off the cling film from the buffet plates, and while everyone was helping themselves I sidled up to Mike.

Out of the corner of my mouth I asked him, 'What time did they ring from the riding school?'

'I don't know, honey. Just before your dad arrived, I think,' he said.

'Well, that's funny. They should have phoned me back by now,' I said.

Now I was really worried, so I left Mike fielding the drinks, grabbed the phone and slipped into the bedroom, out of sight.

'Hello? It's Gillian. Any news about Sadie?'

'I'm not sure,' came the hesitant reply. 'Sara's not back from the field yet and now Ruth has gone up there as well.'

'Oh dear,' I said. 'They should've been back by now. I wonder what's keeping them. I'm right in the middle of this luncheon party I'm having, otherwise I'd be on my way over.'

'Well, we don't know what's going on yet.'

'Can you ask them to phone me as soon as they get back, please?'

'Will do. Bye.'

The throb of the base from the chill-out music seemed to go right through my head as I sat on the bed, agitated. A sense of dread crept over me, sending a shiver down my spine. What was taking them so long?

I caught Mike's eye as I rejoined my family and mouthed silently 'no news'. I slapped a bit of ham on my plate, together with a gherkin and a buttered roll and moved it around on the textured surface for appearances' sake, but I had no appetite. I had one ear on the conversation and the other listening intently for the phone. Yet when the phone did ring, it made me jump, sending a rush of adrenalin through my system that made my hands tremble.

I slipped off into the quiet of our bedroom again, to take the call. It was the yard owner.

Without preamble she said, 'Sadie's hind leg has given out. We couldn't get her up onto her feet. It took two of us over half an hour, rocking her backwards and forwards, to pull her to her feet. Initially she couldn't put any weight on it so we had to wait for her to put it to the ground before we could move her, and it's taken us all this time to get her back to the yard. We've put her in a stable for the time being but I'm concerned about leaving her there. If she goes down in the stable, there's no room for manoeuvre and we'll never get her up again.'

There was a pause in the conversation while I tried to take in the gravity of the situation. I listened to the thump, thump, thump of blood pulsing through my temples as the next words slammed into my chest like a physical blow and churned my stomach to a pulp.

'Gillian,' came those softly spoken words. 'Can we have your permission?'

I thought I knew what she meant but I couldn't believe what was happening.

'My permission? My permission for what?'

'I need your permission to have Sadie put down.'

'Oh no, not my Sadie, not my Sadie,' I cried in anguish. 'Surely there is something we can do for her; there must be something we can do?'

I heard the owner take a deep breath as she measured her words in response.

'Everything that could possibly be done for Sadie has been done, you know that... don't you? And you know what the vet said about her condition slowly deteriorating. Well, now it's time to let her go, and the best thing that you can do for Sadie is to end her pain. Love has its own responsibilities and knowing when to let go, no matter how much it hurts, is the greatest act of love that we can perform.'

I tried to speak but no words came out as the tears coursed down my face and my body shook with silent despair.

'Gillian? I'll take care of everything but Sadie is your horse and I can't do anything without your permission,' came the haunting request.

'I don't want her to suffer,' I sobbed.

'She won't suffer. But she will if you don't give your consent.'

So I gave the only answer I could give and said, 'Yes.'

'I don't know when they'll be able to come, it's a Saturday after all and I don't know if I'll be able to get hold of anyone today, but I'll phone you.'

'I'll come right away.'

'No… don't come now,' the yard owner said. 'I'll phone you, let you know what's happening.'

'I'll wait for your call,' I said.

I just sat there on the edge of my bed, the phone still in my hand, my arms locked around my body, while a strange, hollow whooshing sound echoed in my head, like the sound you get from large seashells on the beach when you press them to your ear. I felt dazed by the suddenness of it all. I knew there would come a time when Sadie would no longer be able to carry on, but I thought that I would have had more warning, that I would have seen it coming. I couldn't take it all in; everything suddenly seemed so surreal.

I don't know how long I had been sitting there, suspended in time, but it was probably only a couple of minutes before Mike popped his head round the bedroom door.

'I wondered where you'd gone… what's the matter, darling? It's Sadie, isn't it…?'

I nodded, barely able to talk, and just managed to gasp out the gist of the conversation.

'I'm going to the yard, Mike,' I said.

'But they told you to wait; they said they might not be able to get anyone today. Your family will be going soon – just wait another half an hour or so, then I'll take you myself. I don't think you should be driving while you're so upset.'

'But I can't go back to the party… not now; I can't face anyone at the moment.'

'Yes, you can. Go and wash your face, people are getting ready to go, just put on a brave face for a little bit longer, then we'll go the yard.'

I knew Mike was right. I didn't want to spoil the day when everyone seemed to be enjoying themselves. I sat silently for a while with closed eyes, trying to get control of my emotions, while Mike went back to the lounge and mingled affably with our guests.

I splashed cold water over my face and wandered wearily out of the bedroom, feeling like some sort of automaton that only responded when a button was pressed. Laughter drifted across the hallway from the lounge, so I went into the stillness of our new kitchen where my dad was having a quiet conversation and I could sit and pretend I was listening without having to take part.

Gradually most of the family started to leave the gathering, some had a late-afternoon shopping trip planned and others were going home to get ready for an evening out. I waved them goodbye at the door and, overcome by an irrational fear that I might have missed a call, I surreptitiously checked our phone in the hallway, making sure it had been put back properly and that the connection was still live.

Yet despite the steady tick-tock from the kitchen clock marking the passage of time, the phone sat stubbornly mute on its base, silently belying the hushed activity that, unbeknownst to me, was already taking place at the yard. With only a few people left, and even those preparing to make their move, I pulled Mike aside and pressed the unyielding handset into his palm.

'I can't stand it, honey. Call the yard; find out what's going on. Have they spoken to anyone? And tell them we're on our way.'

'Do you want to speak to them?'

'I can't speak to them,' I said, frightened of what I might hear. 'You do it for me.'

I went back to the quiet of the kitchen and I saw Mike punch the buttons on the phone in the hallway, then slip quietly into his office next door.

I sat motionless, my hands cupping my face, while my dad chatted on. I didn't want to hear what was being said, couldn't bear to listen, yet I found myself straining in an effort to catch some of the conversation through the half-open doorway, trying to pre-empt what Mike would say when he came back to the kitchen. But his voice grew soft and hushed until it was only a muted whisper and my stomach felt like lead.

My dad must have sensed the change in atmosphere because he stopped talking and looked at me quizzically.

'Is anything wrong?'

But I avoided his gaze and stared intently at the half-open door, waiting for Mike.

Suddenly my hearing seemed sharp and acute; I heard Mike replace the plastic handset with a soft click as it touched the base and then his big frame filled the doorway like a cloud, casting a shadow over me and blotting out the sunlight. His brow was furrowed and his expression pained, a mixture of sorrow and anguish for the news he was about to deliver. I held my breath and stared at him, unblinking, as if the sheer intensity of my gaze could stop the words from forming; but they shattered the silence like broken glass tumbling from a mirror, destroying something that could never be replaced in their wake.

'I'm so sorry, darling,' he said. 'It's all over. Sadie is at peace now.'

CHAPTER 44

With my dad sitting beside me at the kitchen table, I broke down and sobbed.

'My Sadie, my Sadie's gone,' I wept.

Mike sank down in front of me, put his arms around me and pulled me towards him as I buried my face in my hands and cried. I cried for her beauty and grace now lost, I cried for all the good times we had shared that would be no more, I cried for her poor, arthritic legs that had failed her just when life was so good, I cried for the injustice of it all and I cried for me, for the part of me that had just been ripped out and for the hole left behind that would always be hers.

She was gone and I would never run my fingers across those dotty spots again, rub her face or pat her neck or fling my arms around her big belly and clasp her to me in the closest thing to an embrace that I could manage.

Mike told me later that the man had come at once to see Sadie to avoid any further distress, that there hadn't really been time for me to get there, and that it was probably for the best because now I could remember Sadie as she had always been.

With the kitchen party now over, the few remaining members of my family hugged me as they left and I felt the stillness fall like a shroud over our bungalow.

As the hours passed, I became consumed by a grief which slid slowly round my body, its icy tentacles squeezing painfully ever tighter. It sapped the breath from my being until there was nothing left inside but a hollow emptiness, and I felt that I'd been plunged into a temporary madness from which there was no escape. I couldn't bear to go to the riding school, to see the vacuum left behind, and I sat at home suspended in a fog of disbelief, trying to grasp the fact that she was actually gone.

In a dreadful déjà vu of those first few nights prior to Sadie's purchase, I lay awake that night in turmoil. But this time, instead of indecision, I felt as if I'd been swallowed up by a great chasm of nothingness. I listened to Mike's steady breathing and took comfort from his warm presence – my rock; always there for me, always supportive of me, always protecting me, yet ultimately, no one can shield another from the reality of death. When death comes calling, we all stand alone.

Unable to take comfort in the oblivion of sleep, I slid out of bed and into the welcoming shadows of the house. I wandered aimlessly through the lounge and sat for a while stroking the cat's head as she lay recumbent on the settee. I watched her stretch and flex her claws in response to my touch, and I envied her her aura of peace and tranquillity; her acquiescent acceptance of the inevitable. I passed through to the kitchen, pausing to sit in the chair where I had taken the decision to forge ahead with Sadie's purchase, and thought how much my life had changed since then.

Sitting there in the dead of night, I remembered the corn field, next to the yard, where the stalks that didn't bend with the wind had been broken and I realised that, maybe, therein lay my mistake. Perhaps I fought too hard against perceived injustices which were just the natural process of life, all part of a complex equation that we were never meant to understand. I could either fight back and be broken by the bitterness of failure, or bend with the breeze of acceptance and watch the rich patterns of life unfold, with curiosity and with hope.

And then I moved on to the study and sat down on the chair in front of the computer where my fingers absently caressed the keyboard. It was here that my grief found expression in their letters and, in the singular silence that exists only in the dead of night, I wrote a requiem for Sadie.

As the darkness deepened, my horse she came to me,
So wild, so proud, so free and true,
She acted like she almost knew
She'd soon be on her way.

In the midnight hour, my horse she came to me,
I saw her glide across the grass,
As I stood still and watched her pass
And walk away from me.

Surrounded by the dark, my horse she came to me,
She blew so gently on my face
And arched her neck so full of grace,
Then softly went her way.

In the dead of night, my horse she came to me,
I saw her ghostly silhouette
And watched her dance a pirouette
Before she sped away.

In my darkest hour, my Sadie came to me,
She neighed and told me not to mourn,
That she'd be with me every dawn
To watch me on my way.

And as the darkness lifted, my mare she came to me,
I watched her rise above the trees
And felt her spirit on the breeze
That wrapped itself round me.

And as I wrote, I found that instead of being haunted by a single shot, that cracked the silence of the night and sent Sadie tumbling to her knees, my mind recalled the real images I held of her beauty and her grace, and the fun times we had shared together. I thought too of all the things I had learnt from her about life and about myself; how she had taught me to accept her failings as a horse with the same equanimity that she had accepted mine as a human. And then I remembered her indomitable spirit; how her courage had fed my own desire to triumph over adversity – whether we actually succeed in the end, doesn't matter… what matters is that we never give up trying.

And very slowly, the spectre of her death was replaced by the vibrancy of her life, the optimism and joy she brought me, the unswerving affection she gave me and the hope of better things to come.

I felt a sense of peace as I finished the last verse of Sadie's requiem. Her presence was part of me, and of Mike too, and always would be. Now I could find the words to describe what Sadie really meant to me; she was about loving something or someone enough to make a sacrifice; for me, Sadie was the missing piece of the jigsaw in my own humanity.

The first chinks of light were starting to lift the night as I quietly slid back into bed next to Mike, cuddled up to his warmth and finally succumbed to the restful blanket of sleep.

CHAPTER 45

onday was 'rest day' for the horses. It was the quietest day on the yard. There would be no lessons, no customers and hardly any staff; with no one to see my grief, I could be anonymous. I couldn't put it off any longer – sooner or later I would have to go to the yard – I needed to go for myself, as well, to seek closure.

Mike took me in his car. I sat motionless, cushioned by the plush leather of the front passenger seat and stared blankly ahead as we pulled up outside the riding school. Mike got out, drew back the cold, heavy iron gates and parked the car on the driveway. As timing would have it, Ben was walking across the yard. It was Ben who had been with Sadie right until the end and did for her what I could never have done. Within four strides he was by my side and wrapped his arms around me.

'She didn't suffer, didn't know anything about it.'

'I loved that mare,' I sobbed.

'Aye, I know. And she loved you,' and with that, he turned on his heels and was gone.

The door to her stable was closed, like it normally was, but there was no white face bobbing forward to greet me. The sight of Sadie's empty stable sent shock waves through me as I went inside to gather up her rugs from the rail, where they hung inanimate and lifeless. I felt like someone whose lover has left them in the night, whose only presence left behind is the smell on the pillow where their head has lain, and I buried my head in Sadie's rugs, just as I would have done to that pillow, and breathed in her smell with my eyes tightly shut against the reality of her death.

Now I was at the yard I felt compelled by the emptiness inside me to see Sadie's field, to feel close to her memory and verify the reality of her passing now that she was gone. It was a crisp day, so Mike and I took a slow stroll up to the field where the other horses were all grazing contentedly, testimony to the old cliché that life goes on regardless. I wrapped Sadie's requiem around a small bunch of pretty white chrysanthemums that I had bought especially for her and tied them to the top of the gate with yellow ribbon. The pages of the poem flapped quietly on the gentle breeze and I said a prayer for Sadie.

And as if nature had orchestrated some invisible cue, Nobelle stopped grazing and wandered slowly over to the gate to see what was going on. She sidled up to us, hoping for a titbit, and seemed to pause for a moment in disappointment when nothing but a pat on the neck was forthcoming. Then slowly she stuck out her long, strong, glossy neck and her soft muzzle quivered as she caught the sweet scent of Sadie's chrysanthemums. In one fell swoop she clamped her rubbery lips right over those pretty flower heads, ripped them off their stalks and devoured the lot.

Back at the yard it was the owner's big arms that enfolded me this time. I asked her a question that I had been puzzling over the last few days.

'When you first saw Sadie… in the field… what made you think that something was wrong?'

'Just the way she was lying there, without moving… and Cleo.'

'Cleo?'

'Sadie was lying down a short distance away from the rest of the herd, and Cleo was next to her, standing over her, guarding her. She never moved from Sadie's side… as if she knew and was looking after her… That's when I thought that something was wrong.'

'I never had the chance to say goodbye,' I sobbed with regret.

'Lots of people never get the chance to say goodbye to their loved ones,' she replied softly. 'And anyway, how do you say goodbye? She knew you loved her. It was in your touch every time you groomed her, in your voice every time you spoke to her; that was your goodbye, your love for her.'

'Sometimes I wonder about God, does He really see the suffering? She was an innocent creature and I feel so angry that her life was cut short by the arthritis that ravaged her body. There was no God looking after her when she needed it most, where is the justice in that?' I cried.

'Oh, but God *was* looking after her,' came the swift reply and I looked up, puzzled. 'He gave her to you, didn't he? Just when she needed someone to understand her, love her and look after her, she found you. You know, we never had you down for a horse owner, yet despite all the difficulties, you cared for her so. You lavished all your time and affection on her, got her the best medical treatment available and gave her a lovely retirement. Oh, someone was looking after her all right, right up to the very end.'

At home I thought about those words, thought back to the apparently random set of circumstances that had all conspired, one after another, to make her mine; how Sadie had come from overseas to England, then to Kent, passed through all her previous owners and finally to me. Was it really that random? Was it what some call fate? Or was it as I said before, just another part of that complex equation of life that I should accept without question?

It was several more days before I could pluck up the courage to return to the riding school; on my own this time. I pulled onto the yard, switched off the engine and sat there in the silent aftermath. Emptiness.

No one on the yard mentioned Sadie, there was nothing more to say. I went aimlessly into the tack room and rummaged through my things in a half-hearted attempt to clean up my redundant grooming kit.

Autopilot kicked in when someone asked, 'Can you give that horse a brush, Gillian? We're a bit pushed for time and she's needed for a lesson. Thanks.'

I picked up a brush from the riding school box and went through the motions, but somehow things just weren't the same.

It was the same at home. I tried to remember how I filled my days before buying Sadie, but I just couldn't, my mind was a blank. Oh, I had plenty of things to get on with as the days slowly passed. There was the shopping, the cleaning, the ironing, the gardening, popping over to see Mum and a hundred and one other little tasks to consider. But life had lost its lustre and I had no enthusiasm for anything. Even my little part-time job, which I had previously enjoyed, had lost its appeal and time seemed to stretch into infinity. What was the point? I didn't need the extra money now that I had no horse to pay for. No horse, no horse…

I was sitting in the kitchen, staring at my cup of tea, when, suddenly, everything became clear, like someone had switched on a light in the gathering gloom. I pushed back my chair and jumped up from the table with new purpose – I would tell Mike when he came home tonight. Now I knew what I had to do.

Where's that telephone number? I know I have that phone number somewhere. Where did I put it? I became almost frantic in my search for that tatty old piece of paper I had written on, all those months ago. There! There it is! Tucked away in the back of the diary, in the drawer by the telephone.

Without a moment's hesitation I picked up the phone and dialled. My heart was thumping as I listened to it ringing, and then I had an awful thought – supposing no one was in.

'Hello?'

Stunned by the sudden answer, I almost couldn't speak.

'Hello?' she said again.

Thank God, someone's there.

'Ann! Oh hello, Ann, it's me. I need another horse, I must have another one. Please tell Paul to find me another horse!'

And that's just what he did.